To
H.S. Harris
qui facit per alium facit per se

Alles erblickt ich im Glass,
Alte und neue Völkergeschichte,
Türken und Griechen, Hegel und Gans,
Zitronenwälder und Wachtparaden,
Berlin und Schilda und Tunis und Hamburg ...

[I see everything in the glass,
Ancient and modern history,
Turks and Greeks, Hegel and Gans,
Citrus groves and military parades,
Berlin and Schilda and Tunis and Hamburg ...]

Heine, *Die Nordsee II*

EDUARD GANS AND THE HEGELIAN PHILOSOPHY OF LAW

ARCHIVES INTERNATIONALES D'HISTOIRE DES IDÉES

INTERNATIONAL ARCHIVES OF THE HISTORY OF IDEAS

143

MICHAEL H. HOFFHEIMER

EDUARD GANS AND THE HEGELIAN PHILOSOPHY OF LAW

EDUARD GANS AND THE HEGELIAN PHILOSOPHY OF LAW

MICHAEL H. HOFFHEIMER

University of Mississippi Law School

Springer Science+Business Media, B.V.

A C.I.P. Catalogue record for this book is available from the Library of Congress.

ISBN 978-90-481-4503-4 ISBN 978-94-015-8523-1 (eBook)
DOI 10.1007/978-94-015-8523-1

Published by Kluwer Academic Publishers,
P.O. Box 17, 3300 AA Dordrecht, The Netherlands

Kluwer Academic Publishers incorporates
the publishing programmes of
D. Reidel, Martinus Nijhoff, Dr W. Junk and MTP Press.

Sold and distributed in the U.S.A. and Canada
by Kluwer Academic Publishers,
101 Philip Drive, Norwell, MA 02061, U.S.A.

In all other countries, sold and distributed
by Kluwer Academic Publishers Group,
P.O. Box 322, 3300 AA Dordrecht, The Netherlands.

Printed on acid-free paper

CONTENTS

PREFACE

Gans ranks at the head of that important group of Hegelian thinkers that bridged the generations of Hegel and Marx.[1] Yet there is a large gap between Gans's historical importance and the scholarship on him. Despite a renewal of interest in Gans's work on the Continent,[2] Gans remains almost completely unknown to English-language scholars, and almost none of his work has been previously translated.[3] His Prefaces to his posthumous editions of Hegel's writings are inaccessible to English speakers, despite the fact that they shed important light on the authenticity of the so-called Additions to those texts. His Preface to Hegel's *Philosophy of Law* has never been translated before, while his Preface to the *Philosophy of History* has been omitted from reprintings for generations.[4]

Moreover, the recent scholarship on the Continent has focused on Gans's political and philosophical rather than his legal writings. There is little discussion in any language of his system of law, which is the focus of the present study.

Some of the reasons for the neglect of Gans are obvious. Gans cannot be a hero for most readers today. He accepted apostasy as a means to professional advancement. And though more liberal than Hegel, Gans nonetheless accommodated himself to the results of the Restoration and evaded political persecution that might have kindled the sympathy of later generations.

By disclaiming originality in his scholarship, Gans also deterred interest in his works by twentieth-century historians of ideas who have prized innovation and originality. The content of his writings further deterred interest: his ambitious original research on the history of the law of succession remained unfinished, and was so detailed, descriptive, and dated that it would appeal only to the legal specialist or dedicated antiquarian. His principal research interests, Roman Law and the law of succession, were topics that remained peripheral to the interests of ensuing generations of legal historians.[5] On the other hand, his polemical tracts were embarrassingly superficial, repetitious, and vindictive.[6]

For Victor Hugo the idea of translating Gans into French provided the perfect example of tiresome, dispiriting intellectual work. In a scene that may have recorded Hugo's own early efforts to translate Gans,[7] Hugo recounted how a law student struggles to translate Gans. The student takes a daily walk, hoping the exercise will fortify him for work on his translation.

> . . .the work he had on hand at that time was the translation into French of a celebrated quarrel between two Germans, the controversy between Gans and Savigny; he took Savigny, he took Gans, read four lines, tried to write one of them, could not, saw a star between his paper and his eyes, and rose from his chair, saying: "I will go out. That will put me in trim."
>
> And he would go to the Field of the Lark.
>
> There he saw the star more than ever, and Savigny and Gans less than ever.
>
> He returned, tried to resume his work, and did not succeed; he found no means of tying a single one of the broken threads in his brain; then he would say: "I will not go out tomorrow. It prevents my working." Yet he went out every day.[8]

As early as 1826 Heine had caricatured both Gans's ponderous prose and his esoteric research interests in the nightmarish fantasy of an opera with a libretto by Gans about inheritance law and set to music by the contemporary Italian Spontini.[9]

Gans championed three losing causes and in the end he suffered the fate of losers. First, he championed the cause of codifying German civil law at a time when the codification movement was decisively rebuffed. The codification that eventually occurred a half century after Gans's death owed little to his efforts. Second, he supported liberal political values at the height of the Restoration. Seeking an accommodation of national aspirations and traditional German political institutions with guarded support for liberty and greater participatory democracy, Gans stood isolated from the main political and ideological currents of the day. Third, he subordinated his career to the project of promoting Hegel's system of philosophy, and interest in Gans accordingly waned with the decline of interest in Hegel.

By defining his own scholarship as an application of Hegelian doctrine to legal study, Gans sought to expand the influence of Hegel's philosophy in his university lectures, in time consuming work on behalf of the Hegelian Society for Scientific Criticism, and in preparing posthumous editions of Hegel's own writings. Gans succeeded in a short period in rising to a position of preeminence among Hegel's academic followers. But he rose just at the moment that Hegel's reputation, having peaked, began a bumpy decline.[10] Gans – ever ambivalent and accommodating – championed a sort of liberal, centrist interpretation of Hegel that was to be lost in the dynamic debates among Left and Right Hegelians that dominated the period after Hegel's death.

* * *

The present study of Gans hopes to establish that his writings on law and legal philosophy merit closer attention than they have received. These writings provide some of the best surviving evidence of the coverage of legal education at the University of Berlin during the important period before 1848. The translation of his *System of Roman Civil Law* included in this study is, as far as I know, the only German law textbook from that period that is available. The features of Gans's work that account for its lack of appeal to scholars nevertheless shed light on characteristics and limitations of German academic law in the early nineteenth century. The abstract, philosophical, and historical focus of German legal education, evident in Gans's work, manifested the chaos and impotence of private law throughout German states. But the gulf between German academic scholarship and contemporaneous legal practice should not obscure the fact that Gans's legal writings expressed a theoretical response to pressing legal and political problems of his day. His passionate interest in specific doctrinal areas, such as the law of possession, likewise expressed his underlying concern with the practical problems resulting from the absence or inefficacy of private law remedies. Quite apart from the ideological debates about romanticism in law, all educators (including Gans) found their work turning to one of two extremes: on the one hand, they turned to historical reconstruction of details of particular legal practices. On the other hand, they engaged in constructing various systems in laconic prose marked by pervasive abstraction and ambiguity.

Gans's work shared the characteristic defects of the German legal scholarship of his age. It not only failed to provide a mechanism for integrating academic law and legal practice; it discredited the very possibility of academic participation in social criticism and political reform. Strategies of abstraction and ambivalence pervaded the scholarship of Gans and his contemporaries and pose the need to reconstruct the context that subtended the discourse and motivated intense legal debate, historical research, and enmity on issues such as the origin and nature of possessory rights in Roman Law. At the same time, the debates over such esoteric issues are of central importance for the intellectual history of pre-Germany precisely because they were the forum in which the critical intellectual debates took place. And the character of intellectuals as a group and their intellectual product were powerfully affected by the nature of the discourse in which they engaged and through which they defined themselves. The very form of intellectual activity in which Gans engaged – the systematic elaboration of Roman Law – provided cohesion and cultural identity to the German legal profession. His lectures and publications served to create and perpetuate at Berlin a tradition of legal scholarship that was continued by later schools of jurisprudence – among them, *Pandektenwissenschaft* and legal positivism – that were often indifferent or even antagonistic to Gans's Hegelian theory.

Gans's work also merits closer attention than it has received because of its importance for understanding the diffusion of Hegel's views. Gans discloses the power of Hegel's influence and the reach of that influence into disciplines and areas of research in which Hegel himself expressed little real interest (or ability). At the same time, a close reading of Gans's work reveals far more originality among Hegel's proselytes than has been usually recognized. Gans's innovations were not limited to filling gaps, extending, or popularizing Hegel's teaching. On the contrary, Gans redefined the contents of Hegel's philosophy of law; he reshaped the systematic form of Hegel's philosophy; and he altered the treatment of legal and historical components of Hegel's system.

Lastly, Gans's work deserves closer study because it represented a positive and creative product of a northern German culture that is often remembered only for its negative legacy. The intellectual history of Gans cannot pretend to be ignorant of the failure of German intellectuals and legal institutions to prevent the rise of Nazi rule. It is easy in hindsight to find the failings of Gans and German liberal legal theory. It is more difficult today to appreciate the positive contributions of Gans to the history of thought. By his death, Gans was a recognized authority on Roman Law and the history of the law of succession. Hegelian influence no doubt encouraged certain dogmatic views, but it also validated a comprehensive polyglot conception of law which encouraged Gans to acquire a more sophisticated grasp of English and Scots law than any British thinker of the day would acquire of German law. So, too, his history of medieval French law would be translated into French. Gans provided a sounder systematic framework for the Digest than Thibaut, upon whose treatment of Roman Law nineteenth century barristers lavished the most extraordinary praise.[11]

ACKNOWLEDGMENTS

I am very grateful to Norbert Waszek and James Q. Whitman who encouraged my research, read drafts of this work, and provided detailed, helpful criticism. I reconsidered, altered, and qualified several arguments as a result of correspondence with them. Conversations with Robert Haws led me to amplify certain discussions. John Farrow Matlock provided meticulous research assistance and educated me about problems in Latin and Hebrew; the translation of the *System of Roman Law* silently incorporates his corrected citations to the *Digest*. I thank Carmen Shindala, Sara M. Falkinham, and Patricia K. Buffington for proofreading.

Research was supported by a Henry M. Phillips Research grant in jurisprudence from the American Philosophical Society and by summer research grants from the Lamar Order, University of Mississippi Law School. I thank those institutions and their donors.

Michael H. Hoffheimer
Oxford, Mississippi
1995

CHAPTER 1

THE PHILOSOPHY OF LAW OF EDUARD GANS

1.1. Life and Career

> I have laboured carefully, not to mock, lament, or execrate, but to understand human actions ...
>
> *Spinoza*[12]

Eduard Gans was born in 1797[13] into a prosperous Berlin Jewish family. He grew up in years marked by prolonged political and military turmoil, the rise and fall of empires, and the permanent shifting of national state power alignments within the German-speaking world. An infant when the French imperial expansion began, he was a child when the Holy Roman Empire of the German nation collapsed and a teenager when the "War of Liberation" culminated in the French retreat from Eastern Europe and the fall of Napoleon.

Both his personal life and his intellectual development were informed by a sense of his awkward fit into his historical period. As a Jew raised in an alien culture – one that reacted with increasing hostility towards Jews as he grew to manhood – Gans defined his personal and intellectual identity in a way that sought to respond positively to the dominant culture and to redefine that culture so as to encompass heterogeneity. The powerful appeal of Enlightenment ideals and the promise of a liberal state led him eventually to seek full assimilation into German cultural life, including religious conversion. But Gans understood, perhaps better than later generations, that his individual conversion was part of a larger process of Jewish assimilation into north German society. Heine converted the same year as Gans, and Gans no doubt viewed this amalgamation of cultures in which he participated as itself imparting further diversity to the dominant culture.[14]

It is tempting to speculate that Gans's later work exhibited attitudes and defenses that he acquired as a Jew raised in a hostile intellectual environment. Numerous scholars have looked for distinctive Jewish features in works he authored after his conversion. At the time of his death, a Jewish newspaper observed that, though the example of his conversion should not be followed,

Gans nevertheless remained a Jew. "In his particular field Gans also remained – we state this quite openly – a Jew."[15] Gans's later convictions might manifest general patterns of thought that Yirmayahu Yovel identifies as characteristic of Marrano intellectuals: "a this-worldly disposition, a split religious identity, metaphysical skepticism, a quest for alternative ways to salvation that oppose the official doctrine, an opposition between inner belief and the outer world, and a gift for dual language and equivocation."[16] The problem, of course, is that such broadly defined patterns of thought mark modern and post-modern European culture in general. For example, Gans's profound gift for equivocation, manifest so strikingly in his Preface to Hegel's *Philosophy of Law*, was a trait he shared fully with Hegel.

Gans gave voice to his feeling of awkward fit with his age, and in particular his age's resistance to historical progress. He observed in 1828 in a lecture:

> This is the history of the modern period in general. All other histories paused at the time of the French Revolution. One could only consider their influences on the other states, and history took its starting point from France. But because of its many outrages and horrors, a hatred set in after the Restoration towards this event, the foundation of our entire history. And I cannot agree with the view, as little as I can with the fear, that the *ancien regime* will return after the Restoration. Never in history does something return in the same condition. One can neither revere nor fear one's age; one must observe it.[17]

His final injunction – that one must engage in the passive process of observing or contemplating (*betrachten*) – demanded something more than historical verisimilitude. Observation furnished Gans with a strategy for personal survival; and the role of observer deeply shaped his identity and activity as a scholar and teacher. In the role of detached observer he also wrote actively as a cultural critic, literary essayist, and political journalist.[18]

The conclusion in the 1828 lecture – that one "can neither revere nor fear one's age" – comprises a tacit reference to a famous statement by Spinoza[19] and thus further disclosed Gans's sense of detachment from his age at the same time it signified his community with other philosophers (like Spinoza) who had been similarly detached. The reference to Spinoza three years after his formal conversion to Christianity may suggest that Gans continued to see himself as part of a tradition of Jewish intellectual activity. But the image of Spinoza more certainly served as an emblem for radical rationalism and humanism.

Gans belonged to the generation between Hegel and Marx – living in the years between the end of the Enlightenment and the emergence of modernist thought. He attended university in the years immediately after the "War of Liberation" and completed his academic legal education in three years of study. He attended the University of Berlin for three semesters (summer 1816 to 1817). While a student at Berlin, Gans became active in a circle of Jewish intellectuals who met weekly to discuss a variety of topics. Gans was one of the most active participants in these meetings; participants discussed a host of European cultural topics but concerned themselves especially with Jewish issues.[20] His interest in law was reflected in his presentations on "the upcoming lectures on the characteristics of Roman law" and "on the characteristics of public and private legal relationships of Rome."[21]

After Berlin Gans studied law at the University of Göttingen from October 1817 through the summer of 1818. He left Göttingen in August 1818 to enroll in the law faculty at the University of Heidelberg, where he completed his dissertation on the law of forfeiture in the Roman Law of contracts in 1819.[22]

At Berlin and Göttingen Gans was immersed in the legal culture dominated by the so-called Historical School. Public interest in the Historical School was peaking just at the time Gans began his legal studies, and the University of Berlin was home of its most famous and active spokesman, Friedrich Carl von Savigny (1779–1861). Savigny had taught at the University of Berlin since its founding in 1810, and he had been active as a scholar for years. Most recently, only two years before Gans enrolled at Berlin, Savigny had caused a major stir by publishing *The Vocation of our Age for Legislation and Legal Science* (1814), a polemical tract opposing codification of German private law.

The Historical School had an equally powerful presence at Göttingen (where Savigny himself had once studied). At Göttingen the Historical School could trace its intellectual roots to the work of Gustav Hugo. Indeed, the Göttingen Professor Karl Friedrich Eichhorn together with Savigny and J.F.L. Goeschen co-founded the organ of the Historical School in 1815, the *Journal for Historical Legal Science.*[23]

Gans's decision to complete his legal education at Heidelberg was to have an important effect on his career. Like Berlin, Heidelberg was widely respected as a center of legal learning.[24] But in contrast to the modern state-created university in Berlin, Heidelberg's longstanding preeminence went back to the middle ages; and it could proudly point to Pufendorf's residency at Heidelberg from 1661 to 1668. Despite the reorganization of Heidelberg in the early eighteenth century, its established traditions, and the relative weakness of the local state administration, translated into greater academic autonomy from interference.

While Berlin and Göttingen were associated with the Historical School, the University of Heidelberg was identifed with the most important intellectual, political, and personal opponent of Savigny and the Historical School – Anton Friedrich Justus Thibaut (1722–1840). It was Thibaut's public call for the codification of German law, *On the Necessity of Universal Civil Law for Germany* (1814), that had provoked Savigny's polemical tract against codification that crystallized the romantic movement among legal academics into the Historical School. In jurisprudence Thibaut insisted on a doctrinal study of law that derived its validity from a system of relations and obligations. His approach was deliberately formal and classical, and he resisted the romanticist trend that the Historical School promoted which sought to trace social practices, including law, to national folk roots.[25]

Methodological differences in jurisprudence were bound up closely with ongoing political debate. While Thibaut had emerged in 1814 as vocal partisan of the codification of German private law, the Historical School defined itself in opposition to the precipitate codification of German law.[26] Gans thus moved to Heidelberg in 1818 at a fateful moment, and his exposure to the jurisprudence of Thibaut was to exercise a decisive effect on his intellectual development. Gans's decision to leave Göttingen for Heidelberg in 1818 was probably a function of his political convictions, personal experiences, and legal interests.[27] In 1815 and 1816 the social ferment following the "War of Liberation" generated loosely organized student movements at German universities, spreading from Jena in 1815 to other traditionally protestant universities, including the University of Heidelberg. The student activists, encouraged by some faculty members, combined nationalist aspirations and liberal protests against the suppression of free thought. The movements had almost no following among students at Berlin and Göttingen, who were more conservative,[28] and Gans may well have been attracted by Heidelberg's reputation as a center of student activism. While in Göttingen, Gans responded to anti-Semitic attacks on his family. Professor Rühs, a historian at Berlin, had published a criticism of Gans's father, Abraham Gans (who had died in 1813) for supposedly usurious business deals with von Moltke. Gans's first published first work appeared while he was a student at Göttingen, an open letter responding to the posthumous, anti-Semitic attacks.[29]

It was not unusual for German students to attend various universities, but Gans's decision to leave two institutions closely identified with the Historical School and to complete his study at Heidelberg reflected his reaction against the politics, values, or jurisprudence of the Historical School. The Historical School's embrace of German nationalism and its ardent subservience to reactionary political tendencies in Prussia appealed to anti-Semitic currents in the popular culture. Though many discussions of Savigny politely avoid treating his hostility to Jews, he made no secret of it, and when he assumed positions of political and legal power in the 1820s, he worked to oppose and actually reverse the process of Jewish legal emancipation.[30] Anti-Semitic fervor motivated at least some students attracted by the Historical School's nationalist rhetoric. One student of Savigny and Eichhorn in 1820 defended the "thesis" that it was immoral to grant the doctor of laws degree to Jews.[31]

Jews at Heidelberg, too, suffered legal disabilities, but Jews were treated far better there than at Berlin or Göttingen. By 1818 Thibaut "had gained a national reputation as a defender of Jewish emancipation and as the most eloquent opponent of the narrow nationalism and conservative historicism of the Historical School."[32] The students at Heidelberg also exhibited less hostility to Jews and were less receptive to anti-Semitic hate mongering. In 1819 Thibaut led his students in defending Jews in Heidelberg from public attack in 1819.[33]

On March 6, 1819, Gans defended his doctoral dissertation with honors. On March 23, 1819, a deranged student with liberal associations attacked and killed a conservative playwright, providing German state authorities with the pretext for a savage crackdown on dissent. The assassination sparked a period of extensive, and remarkably successful, state censorship and thought control. The political repression was formally institutionalized under the Carlsbad Decrees, by agreement among various German states in September, 1819.[34]

In response to the political reaction and the increased persecution of Jews, Gans and other Jews founded the Union for the Culture and Science of Jews.[35] Gans played a leading role in the Union, serving as Secretary (1820) and President (1821), until its dissolution in 1824.[36] At first the goals of the organization were politically ambitious, as appears from its original name, the Union for the Improvement of the Condition of Jews in the German Federated States.[37] But the persistence of the reaction led to an erosion of optimism, and intellectuals throughout the German states responded to the repressive political atmosphere by turning inward. German Jewish intellectuals, too, redefined their aspirations in more politically ambivalent fashion and in more spiritual terms: the Union sought in the science of Jews "to present the Jewish world to itself," and it defined the culture of Jews as "the inner concept of the collective relations, property, and production of Jews with respect to religion, philosophy, history, law, literature in general, civil life, and all human affairs."[38]

Gans's presented three Addresses to the Union, and the evolution of his views in the addresses document the impact of Enlightenment ideas on Gans's vision of cosmopolitan Jewish culture. At the same time, the addresses document his growing frustration with and distance from the Jewish intellectual community. His earliest address (1821) already reveals some Hegelian influence,[39] but it does not yet identify Gans as a committed Hegelian.[40] The second address (1822) reveals a liberal Jew coming to embrace Hegel as the spokesman for cosmopolitan German culture that was viewed optimistically as growing increasingly indifferent to the distinction of Jew and Christian.[41] A close reading of the second address further reveals a masterly adoption of equivocating postures towards the issue of Jewish assimilation. Gans recognizes as legitimate the universalizing European demand for Jewish integration into the dominant culture. He calls for the merger of Jewish world into the European but qualifies: "To merge does not mean to perish [*aufgehen ist nicht untergehen*]. Only the obstinate, self-centered independence of the Jews will be destroyed, not that element which becomes a part of the whole. . ."[42] In a provocative image, Gans likened the assimilation of Jews to a river flowing into the sea: ". . . neither the Jews will perish nor Judaism dissolve; in the larger movement of the whole they will seem to have disappeared, and yet they will live on as the river lives on in the ocean."[43] While still active as a leader of the Union, Gans voiced his disdain for "studies of ignorant, prejudiced rabbis, who conceived of Judaism not as a part of the whole, but as exclusive and isolated from other branches of knowledge."[44]

The success of the Restoration's program of enforced ideological conformity was due in large part to its avoidance of outright suppression of intellectual dissent in favor of a combination of censorship (that enforced an interior sense of perpetual state supervision) together with an effective monopoly of academic opportunities that allowed the state to co-opt potential dissidents. Having obtained a law degree at a time when opportunities for Jews in legal practice were extremely limited, Gans's only real opportunity lay in an academic position. Although education at pre-college level was controlled by the Church and thus closed to Jews, the emancipation edict of 1812 had announced that academic positions were open to Jews. But Gans's application in 1822 for the position of professor of law at the University of Berlin provided an opportunity for the King personally to declare that Jews were no longer eligible for academic appointment.[45] And Gans accepted a travel stipend as compensation.[46]

In early 1822 Gans still expressed interest in the idea of establishing a Jewish colony in America. Heine jokingly named its capital "Ganstown."[47] But from 1822 to 1824, Gans became further alienated from the political aspirations of those Jewish intellectuals who responded to the political reaction with a separatist or utopian schemes, and who abandoned the cosmopolitan goals of Jewish culture and the political goals of complete legal emancipation. Like other German Jews of his generation, assimilationist social convictions and universalist religious beliefs coincided with personal career aspirations, and Gans formally converted to Christianity in December, 1825.[48] With this conversion he became eligible for the position of professor in the law faculty at the University of Berlin. He was accordingly appointed extraordinary professor in 1826, and he held the position of regular or full professor from 1828 till his death.[49]

Gans had been an associate of Hegel's before his formal conversion. In the years that followed he became Hegel's closest companion. At the same time that Gans socialized increasingly with non-Jews and assimilated Jews,[50] he grew apart from his former Jewish friends. His passion for Hegelianism, legal scholarship, and politics formed the exclusive topics of his autobiographical note and seem to have displaced his former activism in behalf of Jews.[51] One sad result of the politics of accommodation and Gans's quest for assimilation into a culture that defined itself in excluding Jews was his participation in 1838 in signing a petition opposing the promotion of Jews in law faculties.[52] So, too, in a polemic published in 1839, Gans meant to insult romanticism in Roman Law scholarship by likening it to rabbinical scholarship,[53] thus offering a glimpse of those aspects of Jewish culture that repulsed him while displaying his willingness to exploit the pervasive hostility towards Jews in his attack on Savigny.

Gans's lectures at Berlin mirrored his scholarly interests. His first two courses in 1826 were on the Law of Succession and the History and Institutions of English Law.[54] His early interest in Roman Law led to regular lectures on the Digest, Institutes, and History of Roman Law.[55] His abiding interest in the law of succession led to repeated offerings of that course.[56] Interests in history and politics led him to lecture on the history of modern public law. Interest in a universal history of law led to a course on Universal History of Law or the Legal History of the Orientals, Greeks, Roman, Middle Ages and Modern Time (1830).[57] Gans became one of the foremost experts on legal philosophy at Berlin, and he lectured on Natural Law or Philosophy of Law in Relation to Universal History of Law from 1827 through 1830.[58] Gans also announced lectures on Natural Law for the Winter Semester, 1831, but when Hegel's own course on the Philosophy of Law was undersubscribed, Gans cancelled his lectures out of deference.[59] (The incident led to a riff with Hegel, which is discussed more fully below.)

Gans visited Paris in 1830 and experienced the July Revolution.[60] His sympathetic treatment of the revolt led him to become widely viewed as a liberal political figure in opposition to the status quo; his public lectures attracted crowds of 1500 people.[61] Gans promoted a liberal interpretation of Hegel's legal and political philosophy. His struggle to prevent Hegel's ideas from being coopted by reactionary or conservative thinkers is evident, for example, in his Preface to the second, posthumous edition of Hegel's *Elements of the Philosophy of Law*. Gans insisted that the accommodationists fundamentally misunderstood Hegel's identification of the real and the actual.[62] Toews aptly remarks that for Gans "the Hegelian system provided not a reconciling comprehension of an achieved peace, but a critical standpoint for historical orientation within the ongoing dialectical conflicts of the present."[63] Gans enlisted Hegel as authority for the liberal position in important legal and constitutional debates; for example, Gans had been concerned since 1826 with the prospect of Prussian abolition of jury-type trials in the Rhine territories, which enjoyed legal systems modeled after the French civil code.[64] Accordingly, he took pains to point out Hegel's more progressive political views in his Preface to Hegel's *Elements of the Philosophy of Law*: "To mention only a few examples, did the author in a difficult time not set forth open judicial proceedings, open assembly meetings, and trials by jury as the only institutions appropriate to rationality?"[65] So, too, Gans promoted public legal proceedings and defended the freedom of the press in his own lectures.[66] And, with the declining stature of the Hegelian *Yearbooks*, Gans launched his own periodical, devoted exclusively to the critical discussion of Prussian law reform.[67] Gans argued that the Prussian state was neither an absolute state, nor a paternal state, nor a constitutional state; instead he coined a new classification for it as "a guardianship state."[68] He elaborated the critical political implications of the classification: "A guardianship state, like guardianship itself, only lasts for a limited period of time. The emancipation [of the minor] to a higher and freer status is inherent in its nature: one can deny or postpone the emancipation for a time, but one can not avoid its inevitable result."[69]

After 1830 Gans increasingly promoted a liberal interpretation of the Prussian Constitution that defended the need for legal opposition parties.[70] And in devoting increasing attention to the need for the state to respond to the problems of mass poverty, Gans revealed the influence of Saint-Simonian ideas and imparted a critical and social component to Hegelian doctrine.[71] Karl Marx enrolled in Gans's lectures on Criminal Law (1836–37) and the Prussian Civil Law (1838).[72] Waszek has concluded that Gans influenced Marx and that "Marx's writings contain echoes of Gans's ideas and formulations."[73] In the absence of more direct evidence of Gans's influence on Marx, historians will probably never achieve a satisfactory reconstruction of that important link in intellectual history. But regardless of Gans's personal impact on the development of Marx's political thought, Gans played an extremely important historical role. Gans embraced the political middle: "I belong to those people who are devoted to progress, who favor representative monarchy, who oppose the regression to the middle ages, but who at the same time have as little desire for anarchy. I have always not only loved the Middle, that is to say, the true Aristotelian Middle, but I have always taken it for truth itself."[74] One of the most prominent of Hegel's followers at Berlin, Gans promoted a progressive and social interpretation of Hegel's doctrine.[75] Gans thus legitimated and prepared the way for a radical and critical application of Hegel's thought to the political problems of the day.[76]

Gans did not survive to witness the intellectual historical consequences of his elaboration of Hegel's political philosophy. He suffered a series of strokes beginning in the summer of 1838 and died May 5, 1839, at the age of forty-two.[77]

1.2. Gans and Hegel

> I am living very quietly and see almost no one but Gans, my loyal friend and companion.
>
> Hegel (1826)[78]

Writers have been unable to resist neatly symbolizing Gans's pivotal historical role by depicting him as a student of Hegel and a teacher of Marx. But though he did teach Marx, Gans was never a student of Hegel's.

In order to try to fix as precisely as possible the context and sources of Hegel's influence on Gans, it is helpful to recount the facts in reverse chronology. By doing so, I hope to help shed light on the continuing preoccupation of scholars with Gans's relation with Hegel; to explain the impact that Hegel's philosophy (for better or worse) had on the formation of Gans's scholarly interests; and to identify the limits of our probable knowledge of this crucial aspect of Gans's intellectual biography.

1.2.1. Hegel's Proselyte (1825–38)

In the period following Hegel's death, Gans was prominent among the group of scholars that prepared Hegel's complete works for publication. Gans assumed individual responsibility for preparing the text of Hegel's *Philosophy of Law*[79] and prepared Hegel's lectures on the Philosophy of History for publication.[80]

In the years before Hegel's death, Gans had been one of Hegel's closest friends[81] and intellectual associates. After Gans had been promoted to extraordinary professor at Berlin, he and Hegel effected a sort of division of labor. While Hegel gave up teaching Philosophy of Law, Gans lectured on the subject regularly from 1825 to 1830, and he continued to do so after Hegel's death.[82]

1.2.2. The Supposed Breach with Hegel (1831)

The only serious breach between Gans and Hegel occurred at the very end of Hegel's life. It is important to observe that much of the knowledge of the incident stems from Arnold Ruge, whose criticism of Hegel's conservatism provided a motivation to exaggerate Hegel's differences from Gans; Ruge certainly loosely characterized facts in writing that "it is known that death interrupted the preparation of lectures on the philosophy of right directed against Gans."[83]

Gans had witnessed the July Revolution in France in 1830, and he greeted that revolt with more historical enthusiasm than Hegel.[84] Indeed, Gans's sympathetic treatment of the Revolution supposedly led the Prussian Crown Prince to ask Hegel to resume lecturing on the Philosophy of Law.[85] While Hegel did offer lectures on the philosophy of law in 1831 after meeting with the prince in 1831, it does not follow that he resumed teaching the course only because of political pressures. Such an inference is contradicted by the fact (often overlooked) that Hegel had announced lectures on the philosophy of law the year before, in 1830, though he did not give the course at that time.[86] The strongest evidence for a rift between Hegel and Gans is, ironically, a note that Hegel sent to Gans in 1831 when Gans publicly cancelled his course on the philosophy of law and recommended that students attend Hegel's lectures. Hegel apparently felt insulted by the public notice of rivalry with a junior colleague. Nevertheless, the incident obviously demonstrated Gans's continuing commitment to Hegel. And the two teachers were reconciled at Hegel's deathbed – just two days after Hegel had penned the bitter note to Gans.[87]

Gans's patterned his own lectures on the philosophy of law on Hegel's *Philosophy of Law* (1821). The student transcriptions of Gans's lectures that survive[88] offer a direct view of how Hegel's philosophy was read by his contemporaries. But the lectures pose some serious interpretive problems. First, student transcriptions may not be accurate and must be approached critically. Second, the fact that Gans relied on Hegel's *Philosophy of Law* as text and intended his lectures as a commentary on the text makes it impossible to tell when Gans meant to describe and explain Hegel's views and when he meant to expound Hegel's views as his own. This introduced a pervasive ambiguity into Gans's philosophical discourse.

His lectures closely followed the structure of Hegel's system, organizing the philosophy of law thus[89]:

Abstract formal law
- Property
- Contract
- Wrong

Morality
- Imputing responsibility
- Happiness
- The good

Order based on Custom (*Sittlichkeit*)
- Family
- Civil society
- The state

Nevertheless, Gans's lectures revealed subtle, but significant, differences from Hegel's philosophy of law. Gans expressed some political values different from Hegel; for example, in later lectures Gans proposed social policy to ameliorate the critical problem of poverty.[90] But Gans never elaborated his own views by critically distancing himself from Hegel; on the contrary, neither Gans nor Hegel ever explicitly addressed their differences; the two colleagues were either unaware of such differences, chose to ignore them, or considered them to be entirely compatible with Gans's eminent role as proponent of Hegelian philosophy. There were, nonetheless, fundamental differences that concerned both the general nature of philosophy of law and the treatment of details within the system.

One revealing difference between Gans and Hegel was Gans's insistence on philosophy of law as "Natural Law." Gans entitled his lectures "Natural Law." Hegel, too, had lectured on Philosophy of Law under the title Natural Law (*ius naturae et civitatis*), and Hegel had accordingly also entitled his textbook on the facing title page: *System of Natural Law or Political Science in Outline*.[91] (This alternative title appeared as a subtitle in Gans's posthumous edition, and it is one of the minor scandals of modern scholarship that the translations of the book omit it altogether.) Yet while Gans referred to Hegel's book (in his preface) as *Natural Law*, Hegel himself tended to avoid the term. Gans described Hegel's philosophy as placing natural law after psychology,[92] but Hegel would probably only have accepted the description as ironic. Hegel had used the term "natural law" in 1802–03 in an early critical article, "Natural Law: The Scientific Ways of Treating Natural Law, its Place in Moral Philosophy, and its Relation to the Positive Sciences of Law," but even in 1802 Hegel's view of natural law was ambivalent, and as Acton observed, "Hegel's use of it in the title of this essay is somewhat paradoxical, since he rejects the whole idea that society is deliberately formed by the association of pre-existing individuals. Indeed, he goes further than this and in effect holds that the positive law of each state is more rational and fundamental than any supposed law of nature held to be valid always and everywhere."[93] In Hegel's earliest systems, he associated a philosophy of natural law as part of a philosophy of nature, but by 1807 his system had been transformed several times, the "state of nature" had largely disappeared as subject matter for legal science and had been supplanted by the "state of law."

We may speculate that Hegel associated his philosophy with natural law in later years for two reasons; first, his lectures were scheduled under a conventional part of the curriculum on Natural Law, and it was convenient to transport and expand the coverage of legal philosophy from his Encyclopedia to the traditional course and to adopt its title as an alternative for his textbook; second, Hegel identified ideologically with the legislative objectives of advocates of Natural Law jurisprudence (notably Thibaut), and natural law assumed new and favorable political connotations for Hegel after 1814 when it became associated, through Thibaut, with the codification movement and stood in opposition to the Historical School.

Gans, however, regarded his (and Hegel's) system of legal philosophy unambiguously as an exposition of natural law. This is especially clear in the genealogy Gans provided for the philosophy of laws, where he divided modern legal philosophy into three periods: 1) the foundation of legal philosophy, which included Spinoza, on the one hand, and Enlightenment writers, like Montesquieu and Wolff, on the other; 2) the transformation of legal philosophy, which included Rousseau and Kantians; and 3) the revival of legal philosophy or the "return of natural law to actuality," which included later day proponents of natural law doctrine.[94]

Gans's legal training led him to handle the contents of the system differently from Hegel, though it is never clear how aware he was that he departed from Hegel. Gans's greater knowledge of substantive legal doctrine and his great concern with the law of succession appeared throughout his lectures. Familiarity with doctrinal and practical aspects of law led Gans to treat the components of Hegel's system in more concrete terms, and this shifted the focus of the system as a whole. In general, Gans recast the contents of the system, which for Hegel encompassed many nonlegal social institutions, in much more legal terms.[95] For example, Hegel counterposed the Order based on Custom to the sphere of abstract law, and Hegel's dense transition from Morality to the Order based on Custom made no direct reference to law, legal rights, or legal institutions.[96] In contrast, Gans revealed a far greater interest in the legal doctrines that regulated such social institutions in this part of the system, and he termed it "The Law (*Recht*) of Order based on Custom" in the 1828–29 lectures.[97]

In treating the family under the rubric of Order based on Custom, Hegel included a very abstract and equivocal discussion of inheritance law which (omitting any description of actual laws) invoked the emergence of testamentary succession to explain the dissolution and disintegration of the family with the rise of superior individual legal rights. (sections 178–80.) Gans's system defined the family in narrower legal terms. In other words, while Hegel placed the family as an anthropological phenomenon in the Order based on Custom part of his philosophy of law, Gans limited his corresponding treatment to family *law*. His legalistic reading of Hegel's more abstract, comprehensive, and equivocal discussion was plain from the explanation Gans offered for his organization: "Positive law treats the law of succession as part of the Law of Things, but it necessarily belongs to Family Law."[98]

Gans retained some of Hegel's equivocal language about the dissolution of the family, but Gans completely inverted the meaning of this dissolution. For Hegel the dissolution was fraught with implications of tragic loss of natural spontaneity. Gans recast the dissolution in positive terms as the instantiation of family relationships through legal institutions. He explained, "The law of succession is the dissolution of the family in the sphere of wealth (*Vermögens*). In the law of succession, blood relationship comes into its real existence."[99] This positive treatment of the transition provided an overarching systematic validation of the synthesis of testate and intestate succession that Gans worked to achieve in his treatment of private law.

Gans sketched the history of the law of succession in his lectures for 1828–29 and 1832–33; he presented this history as a progressive development and treated the balance between freedom of testamentary alienation and forced shares as an ethical accommodation between individual freedom and the preservation of the family. For Hegel the disintegration of the family had meant that civil society was bound together as a collection of legal persons,[100] but for Gans civil society was a collection of families – "complex of families"[101] – and Gans radically reinterpreted the disintegration of the family in subjective or psychological terms as the loss of family *feeling*.

From such differences in treatment, it was evident that Gans did not consider Hegel's *Philosophy of Law* to be authoritative either in detail or in its coverage of legal subjects. He followed the sequence of topics carefully, but he altered the meaning of topics by tinkering with the transitions that regulated their relationships to other parts of the system. Gans understood his activity as expounding and developing the system elaborated by Hegel, but the ambivalence of the relationship provided Gans freedom to elaborate his own views as Hegel's.

This ambivalence found full expression in Gans's Preface to the posthumous edition of Hegel's *Philosophy of Law*. While insisting that Hegel's central philosophical arguments had been anticipated by less controversial thinkers, Gans identified Hegel's original contributions to philosophy of law as the establishment of a scientific and systematic expression, the cancellation of the distinction between law and politics, the achievement of a perspective that combines all peculiarities of national history:

> And what an awesome spectacle concludes this book. From the summit of the state individual states are surveyed as just so many rivers flowing into the sea of world history, and the short sketch given of the development of world history does no more than suggest the more important topics that belong to that field.

In defending the work against critics, Gans seized one of Hegel's most deeply equivocal passages – "What is rational is actual and what is actual is rational" – and claimed that, "plainly interpreted," the language did not bear the conservative meaning attributed to it. Yet Gans himself studiously avoided attributing a determinate meaning to these words.

Hegel's system assumed a deep personal meaning for Gans that is hard to reconstruct. Gans linked his identity to Hegel and defined himself intellectually as a participant in the Hegelian system of philosophy much as he defined himself personally as a self-conscious participant, assimilating into European culture. There is a striking parallel between the passage in his Preface to the *Philosophy of Law*, in which he depicts states flowing like rivers into the sea of world history, and the passage in his youthful vision of Jewish assimilation, in which Jews survived "as the river lives on in the ocean."

In 1826, at the same time that Gans began his law lectures, Gans and other followers of Hegel in Berlin established the Society for Scientific Criticism. Immediate causes for the organization included academic politics, but the resulting society institutionalized Hegel's system. Gans devoted much time to the organization. He traveled to Paris, to Munich, and to German university towns to promote the Society.[102] The Society had three classes, and Gans's leading position among Hegel's followers was indicated by the fact that he was named as secretary of the Philosophy Class, which included Philosophy, Theology, Jurisprudence, and Political Science. Gans also served as General Secretary for the whole Society, and his duties included editing, finances, and correspondence. He drafted the bylaws of the Society and would later recall the heated debates that surrounded the adoption of these rules.[103] Gans occupied different positions within the Society, and he played an active role with Hegel in editing the Society's annual publication *Yearbook for Scientific Criticism*, which began to appear in 1827[104] publishing twenty reviews in the Yearbooks from 1827 to 1839.[105]

1.2.3. Gans's Approach to Hegel (1819–25)

Gans's first direct communication with Hegel can be dated back to a conventionally obsequious letter that he wrote to Hegel in October 1823, with which he sent the first volume of *The Law of Inheritance in World Historical Development*:

> It is not without the greatest shyness that I am sending to you the first volume of my book on the law of succession which is now finished after many delays – shyness which anyone would feel upon entering the court of the judge whom he holds to be competent. I have had to acknowledge in the book's Preface how only the study of your philosophy gave rise to the idea of working out the book that I enclose.[106]

(The import of the letter must not be exaggerated, however, for Gans had sent a similarly worded letter to Savigny a few years before.[107]) The first volume of Gans's major work expressed a strong debt to Hegel. Its Preface cited Hegel as well as Hegelian scholars. More important, its goal, a comprehensive rational survey of the law of succession in its development in separate legal cultures (culminating in the present), revealed Gans's enthusiastic adoption of basic tenets of Hegel's systematic and historical approach.

Gans found in Hegel a philosophical perspective that infused his own scholarly preoccupation with importance. Legal history, Gans insisted, necessarily moved towards universal legal history, because to be concrete legal history had to comprehend the totality of the development of the concept of law in time.[108] Gans was to devote much of the rest of his career to work on a multivolume treatise on the law of succession. The scope of this major project – envisaged from its start as the major scholarly effort of Gans's career – evidenced the depth of Gans's commitment to Hegelian doctrine as a valuable aid to organizing and interpreting the historical and legal material. His treatise continued to appear after Hegel's death, but Gans never succeeded in bringing his study home to Central Europe, nor did it ever reach the present.[109]

Despite Gans's enthusiasm for Hegel, his primary research interests in Roman Law and the law of succession predated Hegels influence. Indeed, Gans's understanding of the enduring value of Roman Law – and his concomitant need to reconcile its universality with its history – help to explain the powerful appeal of Hegelian philosophy. The contemporary relevance of Roman Law legitimated its historical study. As he explained in his treatise *On the Study and System of Roman Law*, "We may also count civil law among our debts to antiquity and to the past. When Rome was overcome by the life of the fatherland in private life and fell during the Conquest, civil law found its proper birthplace, and even completed its education."[110]

Because Gans's interest in Roman Law and the law of succession preceded exposure to Hegel, his legal scholarship cannot be dismissed simply as the mechanical application of Hegelian concepts to an existing body of legal materials. The exact opposite may be closer to the truth: Gans's sustained study of problems of legal history led him to embrace certain Hegelian doctrines. The history of Gans's approach to Hegel accounts for Gans's failure to assimilate important terms of the Hegelian vocabulary in his own *System of Roman Civil Law* and explains the striking interpretive departures that we have observed in Gans's lectures on Hegel's system.

Gans's commitment to Hegelian philosophy cannot be established with certainty before 1822; his work on universal legal history grew out of research he engaged in as part of his activity in the Union for the Culture and Science of Jews. His study of Mosaic-Talmudic law of succession in his treatise first appeared in the journal of the Union for the Culture and Science of Jews.[111] Neither the topic itself nor his treatment of sources establish a Hegelian influence in the work. But by 1823 Gans came to define Jewish culture itself in Hegelian terms as the expression of "consciousness of itself."[112]

Hegel's influence cannot be traced back still earlier to Gans's student years in Heidelberg.[113] Hegel had taught at Heidelberg since 1816 and lectured on the philosophy of law in 1817. Hegel also published the first edition of his *Encyclopedia of the Philosophical Sciences* (1817) for the use of his students at Heidelberg. But Gans had no direct contact with Hegel at Heidelberg, because Hegel left Heidelberg just at the time Gans arrived.[114]

Moreover, Gans's work before 1820 is devoid of any language or ideas that can be attributed specifically to Hegel, despite the fact that they express legal interests that Gans was to pursue for the rest of his career. Hegelian terminology (*aufzuheben*) and doctrines (the idea of the family and state) make their first appearance in Gans's Address to the Jewish Union in October 1821.[115]

On the contrary, Gans's treatise *On the Roman Law of Obligations* (1819) incorporated a historical discussion of Roman Law that sought to make some sense of Roman legal classification and that did not exhibit any familiarity with basic Hegelian terms. Its treatment of classification was strikingly un-Hegelian; in it Gans exhibited a preference for dichotomies for the sake of convenience, and his organization was not connected integrally to the contents. He even suggested in one place that one such division was neither exhaustive nor comprehensive.[116] Likewise, his long study of Gaius in 1820[117] had no notes citing Hegel. Most of the text was a close comparative study of Gaius's Institutes, which had been recently discovered. But its longest chapter departed from the commentary format and purported to be "an overview of the whole history of the law of succession." (276) The sequential topical organization of the materials in that chapter and the dichotomy of inheritance law into testate and intestate succession (277–78) confirms the absence of any appreciable Hegelian influence. And, of course, his admiring letter to Savigny in 1819 or 1820 further confirms his distance from Hegel at that time.

Hegel's influence on Gans's approach to law can be dated to sometime between late 1820 and 1822. Precisely because of the date, however, it is difficult to identify the probable source of the influence. At that time Gans had returned to Berlin where Hegel's ideas were widely diffused. Hegel himself was at the university and lectured on the Philosophy of Law from 1817 to 1822. Hegel's major book *Elements of the Philosophy of Law* appeared in January 1821,[118] and Gans later recollected that the book sparked the great turning point in his approach to law: "For me this book first gave the courage to propose a new perspective for the science of law."[119]

From the chronology of Hegel's influence, it appears that Gans embraced Hegelian philosophy at the critical moment in his spiritual and intellectual biography when he struggled to reconcile Judaism with a universal or cosmopolitan view of science and culture. His personal abandonment of the struggle and his decision to assimilate coincided with his striking acceptance of Hegelian doctrine and illuminates its appeal for Gans. The aspiration of Hegelian philosophy to an extremely abstract absolute science and its promise of integrating particular disciplinary studies within an all-comprehensive totality provided Gans with the systematic and theoretical perspective that infused his own particular work with the grander significance that he no longer found in a personal religion.

Gans's address of April 1822 to the Union for the Culture and Science of Jews evinces a passion that suggests powerfully that his comments had strong personal and autobiographical meaning. He scorned the results of most Jewish scholars and acknowledged the value of Christian thinkers in raising the intellectual level of Jewish study. At the same time, he deplored the subservience of Christian scholarship to theology. Although he does not mention Hegel, his demand for independent "science" incorporated implicitly Hegel's perspective:

> The scientific study of Jewish religion, history and philosophy has so far been either bereft of freedom or of independence. The studies of ignorant, prejudiced rabbis, who conceived of Judaism not as a part of the whole, but as exclusive and isolated from other branches of knowledge, did not produce any faithful or credible results... Any credible results [in the field of Jewish scholarship] are mainly due to the efforts of Christian scholars. But while the rabbis lacked the necessary freedom in their studies, the Christian approach to Judaism lacked independence: much too often it

> was turned into a discipline secondary, and merely ancillary, to Christian theology. Our first priority, therefore, ought to be the establishment of an unbiased and completely independent study of the Science of Judaism which will be integrated into the whole of human knowledge. . .[120]

By embracing Hegelian philosophy – the highest expression of European culture but one independent of theology – Gans sought to bring science to Judaism. To employ the provocative image from his address, he simultaneously poured his individual rivulet into the ocean of world and European history.

Conversely, Hegel's abstract and ambivalent treatment of religion in general and of Christology in particular may have eased Gans's decision to convert by justifying an esoteric view of Protestant theology that comported with his own universalist convictions.[121] At the same time, the Hegelian vision of history and society offered Gans a source of community that he lost with his conversion and would probably never find in the dominant culture. The intensity of Gans's personal commitment to the Hegelian organization manifested the deep roots of his identification with Hegel and Hegelian ideas.

Identifying his scholarship with Hegel in 1823 may also have been politically expedient – or Gans may have believed that it was. Called to Berlin in 1817 to fill the chair in philosophy occupied previously by Fichte, Hegel loomed as one of the most respected professors at the institution. Gans no doubt looked to him as an academic authority and may also have considered him to be a prospective patron or protector.

At the time Gans returned to Berlin and converted, Hegel would have appeared as the spokesman for a systematic philosophy identified, albeit obliquely, with liberal politics.[122] Nowhere was this identification established more plainly – nor the debate engaged in more indirectly – than in Hegel's association with the codification movement and his opposition to the Historical School. Hegelian ideas provided a context for Gans's lifework that concealed his critical legal and political values behind a wall of esoteric language. And Hegelian ideas simultaneously raised Gans's dull and academic views to world-historical importance.

A few years before his death, Gans composed an autobiographical notice. Omitting any reference to his religious beliefs or his Jewish origins, Gans identified three main themes in his life: 1) his theoretical interests in law and philosophy and his association with Hegel; 2) his struggle against the Historical School; and 3) his political writings.[123]

1.3. THE VALUE OF ROMAN LAW

As Greece is the land of art, so Rome is the world of law.

Gans[124]

In the early nineteenth century Roman Law assumed a political importance throughout Europe that was out of all proportion to – and, in truth, only tenuously related to – its relevance to specific features of contemporary European legal doctrine. In the German academic world after 1820, dominated by outer censorship and inner suppression of political ideas, debate over points of legal history came to substitute for the expression of political views. The intensity that Gans brought to his study of the history of Roman Law and the fervor with which he championed its value revealed the depth of passion that attached to the ideas behind the issues under academic discussion.

Legal academic culture was remarkably successful in defining itself in a way that prevented the debate from directly engaging in political discourse that could threaten the autonomy and survival of the academy. Intellectual defenses included abstraction, equivocation, and historical detachment. Gans's vision of Roman Law derived its coherence from the function it played in this debate. Four aspects of Gans's valuation Roman Law overlapped and reinforced each other in the debate.

First, the success of Roman Law and its pattern of historical development supported the codification of German law. Gans constructed a very specific vision of Roman Law that derived from the classical Roman Law and especially from the consolidation of Roman Law under Justinian. The exposition of Roman Law in the Digest occupied a privileged position and was viewed by Gans – and others, including Savigny[125] – as the paradigm for a comprehensive codification of private law. Gans's historical vision of Roman Law comported with the legislative and didactic uses to which the vision was to be put. He emphasized substantive doctrine while ignoring ritual and procedure, and he emphasized the rational, systematic, organizational features. Valuing Roman Law as a historical achievement, maintaining its central role in legal pedagogy, insisting on the continuity of its historical influence, discovering the survival of valid Roman legal doctrines in contemporaneous practice – all defenses of Roman Law promoted the desirability and feasibility of codifying German private law.

The question of codification was itself politically charged. The passion evoked by the debate begun in 1814 regarding codification is doubtless explained in part by the association of legal codes with France (which had effectively exported its Civil Code into several German states) and with those rationalistic, cosmopolitan (and Francophile) influences that had prevailed upon the Prussian rulers to adopt a Code in the eighteenth century. Moreover, the Historical School's resistance to legislation rested on an alternative vision of legal authority that legitimated the role of a professorial elite as jurists that was congenial to corporatist and academic values with deep roots in German culture.[126] In this debate the Historical School spoke as the voice of conservatism and nationalism; its opposition to codification in a legal culture that lacked a tradition of judicial autonomy and that was devoid of any practice comparable to English common-law lawmaking was tantamount to a commitment to the legal status quo or at most a guarded support for slow modification of existing legal relations and institutions.[127]

Second, the vision of a state private law that incorporated substantive features of Roman Law provided Gans with a cosmopolitan alternative to a society defined in nativist terms. Establishing the continuity of doctrines of Roman Law countered the politically conservative and nationalistically motivated efforts of the Historical School to discover the roots of German law in native medieval practice. Roman Law also served to promote the autonomy of law, which the Historical School questioned. Gans understood the Historical School as a threat to the autonomy of legal study because of its dependence on material outside law, and he linked this erosion of the autonomy of law to romantic glorification of the Middle Ages. He suggested that the inherent contradictions of romanticist attitudes were most sharply exposed in their application to legal study by the Historical School.[128] "Law, however, which does not have residence in the present but rather is precisely this very present, must be threatened in its existence by the demand to turn away from the present and turn to the past – for this could be nothing but the cancellation of law."[129]

Third, Roman Law promoted cultural values and pedagogical objectives of German classicism and, conversely, challenged the project of the romanticists. Roman Law was one of the best examples of contemporary European culture's debt to classical antiquity, and Gans was conscious of the utility of Roman Law in the defense of classical values.[130] He defined his intellectual activity in broad terms as part of the German classicist movement and associated Hegel's philosophy generally with classicism. In his memoirs he objected to the denigration of the *Yearbooks* of the Society for Scientific Criticism as merely vehicles for Hegel's views, and he emphasized that contributors included Goethe and Wilhelm von Humboldt.[131]

Fourth, the validity of Roman Law over time and across cultures evidenced a body of substantive legal doctrine independent of legislative authorities. This supported a theory of natural law and suggested the possibility of a criterion for the validity of positive law. Gans's effort to defend the validity of Roman Law and the value of its study reflected his abiding concern, which informed all his scholarship, to establish an absolute basis for valid law as distinct from any empirical institution or practice. His insistence on an absolute basis for legal right appeared almost as monomania in his polemics on possession. Gans's passion for Roman Law expressed his passion for a world of legal rules independent of the political power.

Roman Law provided Gans with both the material and the model for a systematic treatment of law. In his *Treatise* he made this didactic purpose of the study of Roman Law explicit: he argued that science (*Wissenschaft*) required the connection of individual legal doctrines, and that "true science is only a system."

> One can, of course, discuss property, contract, marriage, and inheritance without any system; and one can analyze and represent their phenomena; but what property, contract, marriage, and inheritance are can only be comprehended in the arrangement (*Stellung*) that they have to each other. And every untrue and false arrangement immediately imparts to the content and makes the content untrue and false.[132]

The role of Roman Law in the search for the true system exposed a central ambiguity in Gans's theory: Roman Law simultaneously denoted the subject matter and the critical method by which the subject matter was treated. In Hegel's philosophical effort to subsume the treatment of disparate doctrines under a scientific system, Gans thought he found a way of overcoming the gap between existing law and the philosophical study of law. At the same time, the identification of this system with the Code movement promised a legislative vehicle for realizing the principles of abstract law in positive laws.[133]

In opposing the conservatism of the Historical School, Gans looked to the success of Roman Law to support an alternative, systematizing vision of law. His alternative vision was rooted in natural law principles and in turn supported his political objectives of legislative codification. The tendentious, liberal consequences of the neo-classical vision of law obscured the extent to which the vision of legal scholarship of Gans committed him to a view of history that assumed profound historical continuity. Gans did not aspire to establish the legal validity of details of Roman Law for contemporary German private law. He modified substantive features of Roman Law to make it comport with the theoretical and legal needs of the present. His selection, reorganization, and modification of Roman Law principles was radical in places. Nevertheless, the selecting, reorganizing, and modifying, howsoever radical, manifested the continuation of the Roman Law practice of digesting and revising. In this way his *System of Roman Civil Law* was itself an exercise in Roman Law, not only because the subject matter of the system was Roman Law but also because the systematic study was itself a practice of Roman Law jurisprudence. His work on Roman Law ultimately revealed a theme that recurred throughout his scholarship and that united his seemingly unrelated interests in the law of succession, universal history of law, and Roman Law. Study of Roman Law –before and after his conversion – provided continuity and stability in his personal life. And in still larger historical terms Roman Law derived value as a continuous body of doctrine and a parallel practice of scholarly commentary and redaction that reached back across cultural and national boundaries directly to the jurisconsults of Rome. His system of Roman Law mediated past and present by reducing the forms of control exercised by the past over the present to a scientific system.

1.4. The System of Roman Law

1.4.1. Didactic Purpose and Sources

The format of Gans's *System of Roman Civil Law* reflected the system's pedagogical function as a syllabus for Gans's lectures on Roman Law in 1826–27.[134] His outline provided students a convenient overview, summary, and didactic presentation of substantive doctrines of Roman Law, arranged in a comprehensive fashion. The outline also provided a source book or anthology for students, because its 201 footnotes contained extensive and generous quotations of the Latin text of relevant Roman Law sources, mostly the Digest.

In contrast to hundreds of citations to the Digest, the System referred to or quoted the Code thirty-three times[135] and the Novels twice[136]; it quoted or cited the Institutes only eleven times.[137] The Institutes of Gaius was cited but once,[138] which may be surprising in light of Gans's intensive research on that text. Cicero was cited once.[139] I have been unable to identify the source of one quote.[140]

The contents of the system reflected the convergence of the two main influences on Gans's intellectual development: Thibaut and Hegel. The Digest had, of course, been a focus of legal learning on the continent for centuries; but Thibaut had shifted the study of the Digest from regarding it passively as a source of legal doctrine into manipulating it more actively as a valid taxonomic construct for legal thought. Gans treated the problem of legal structure as an appropriate exercise for applying Hegelian philosophy to a well established part of the legal curriculum. The result was a radical selection and reworking of the subject matter from the Digest itself. Gans's aggressive reorganization of material from the Digest is illustrated by the sequence of passages he excerpted. For example, the second chapter of *System of Roman Civil Law* cited material from the Digest in the following sequence. (I have omitted two citations to the Code.)

50.17.209
50.17.32
1.5.14
1.5.7
50.16.231
1.5.10
50.16.1
50.16.195
5.1.12
50.13.5
50.16.42
37.15.2
3.2.20
34.5.9
35.2.68
50.1.25
49.14.6, 37
3.4.1
4.2.9
4.3.15
43.16.4
22.6.1, 2, 3, 7, 8, 9

In only two places did Gans here follow the sequence of his source.

Comparison of Gans's organization with the sequential treatment of the corresponding material in the Institutes of Justinian confirms also that Gans did not follow the classical Roman Law pedagogy. His system departed significantly from the Roman Law systematic architectonic of Persons, Things (property, contract, and delict), and Actions. The scope of reorganization and differences in coverage of comparable topics can be shown schematically (with the caveat that the numbered sections of the Institutes vary in length):

(book section)	*Institutes* (section numbers)	Gans's *System*
paternal power	1.9	325–45
marriage	1.10	300–24
guardianships (all)	1.13–1.26	346–62
types of property	2.1–2.9	92–189
succession	2.10–2.25, 3.1–3.12	363–441
obligations generally	3.13	190–96, 286–99
contract	3.14–29	197–267
delicts	4.1–4.5	268–84
actions generally	4.1–4.18	55–91

Gans was not the first German legal scholar to attempt to provide a new systematic framework for the substantive Roman Law contained in the Digest. Gans shared the assumption of his contemporaries that the Digest provided the most authentic source for doctrinal Roman Law. But his critical reworking of material also manifested the assumption that the classical organization of legal doctrine in the Digest and Institutes did not provide a wholly adequate system for understanding Roman Law. Legal science, as systematic study, required fashioning a new arrangement and classification of the material.

Gans thus radically reworked the material, departed from the conventional arrangements, and succeeded in elaborating a superstructure for the system that effectively related the components at the same time that it justified the autonomy of the study and related it to other subjects. His achievement contrasted favorably with Thibaut's previous efforts to systematize the law of the Digest. Gans's departure from Thibaut was all the more surprising in that Gans openly admired Thibaut and repeatedly evoked Thibaut as authority.[141]

Thibaut had first published his *System of the Law of the Pandects* in 1803, and further editions appeared in 1805, 1808, 1813, 1817, 1822, 1828, 1835, and (posthumously) 1845.[142] The frequency of appearance of new editions suggests that Thibaut meant his work for use as a text by law students in connection with his lectures. Thibaut justified his organization at least in later editions, on pedagogical grounds,[143] but his architectonic differed from Gans's and preserved more completely the traditional threefold organization of Roman Law as the law of persons (understood as status), things (understood as rights), and actions (understood as legal process):

Thibaut's Organization

Universal Part
Particular Part
- I. Governmental law
  - 1) Cameral and Finance law
  - 2) Police power
    - A. Paternal power
    - B. Guardianship
- II. Private Law
  - 1) Rights in things
  - 2) Personal rights
- III. Legal Procedure as mixture of private and governmental law

Though Gans included an introductory treatment of law in general, he did not divide his subject into a general and particular part. He omitted any separate treatment of public or governmental law, because his system was defined as a system of private law *and* because he treated public law in other courses. Unlike Thibaut (and Justinian), Gans placed legal procedure (as the realization of law) before his treatment of doctrines of private law. Where Thibaut placed paternal power and guardianship as components of state law, Gans treated them as part of private law under the family just prior to the law of succession.

By comparing Thibaut's and Gans's treatments of guardianship, it becomes evident that Thibaut followed the schematic organization of the Institutes far more closely than Gans. For example, the Institutes treated various types of guardianship at the end of Book I (the law of persons)[144] and Thibaut, too, placed Guardianship directly between paternal power and the law of things. In contrast, Gans included guardianship with family law but moved both out of the first part, and he moved family law after property law and just before the law of inheritance. This changed the system as a whole. By moving family law, the law of persons was deprived of its most significant contents and effectively eliminated as an autonomous component of a system. Moreover, by placing family law between delicts and succession, Gans meant to treat family law as private law, and not as public law, as had Thibaut.

There are two plausible motives for Gans's reorganization of guardianship. First, the institutions of guardianship, like the English uses and trusts, played a vital role in the disposition of property after death. A full treatment of Roman Law of succession necessarily required a consideration of various guardianship relationships, and the traditional separation of such relationships from the law of testate and intestate succession would have appeared arbitrary to someone, like Gans, who was concerned with expounding the substantive Roman Law of succession as a coherent whole. Second, Gans may have been encouraged to treat family law and guardianship after the private law of property, contracts, and delicts because of Hegel's location of the family, as part of order based on custom, after the treatment of private law, as part of Abstract Law. For Hegel inheritance law played a prominent role in the transition from the law of the family to civil society. Hegel depicted the law of intestate succession as manifesting the natural dissolution of the family, and he depicted the legal recognition of testamentary devices as manifesting the subordination of this natural family process to the arbitrary will of the individual legal person.[145]

Gans had a different audience for his system than Thibaut, and the objectives of the two systems reflected this difference. Where Gans prepared his system as a textbook and anthology, Thibaut composed an academic treatise on Roman Law. Thibaut's discussion assumed familiarity with the substance of the Digest on the part of the reader; his extensive annotations were designed to provide critical commentary on commentators rather than to provide citations to relevant Digest texts.

Thibaut's effort to present the law of the Digest in a systematic form reflected his personal conviction that law must be arranged coherently according to internal features of legal doctrine – rather than arranged historically, with a concomitant accidental and chaotic presentation of doctrine. Thibaut's interest in reducing Roman Law to a systematic exposition was consciously associated with his political commitment to codifying contemporary German laws.[146] Thibaut also designed his work on the Digest as a comprehensive discussion of basic issues in jurisprudence. For example, he commenced the work with a characteristic Enlightenment discussion of the difference between natural and human laws, and the difference between moral and legal laws.[147] Such a general discussion – familiar to English readers from the preliminary part of Blackstone's *Commentaries on the Laws of England* – was entirely absent from Gans's system, which defined its topic in narrow legal terms and began immediately with common civil law.

The more explicit educational purpose of Gans's system is evinced by his specific treatment of matters such as reference works (sections five and seventeen), the textual sources of Roman Law (section seven) and its historical stages (section six). There is no comparable treatment of such basic topics by Thibaut. On the other hand, Gans includes a reflective discussion on methodology (sections one through three), which has no counterpart in Thibaut. The differences between Gans's and Thibaut's treatment of general legal principles is evident from the sequential placement (by section number) of those topics which the two systems treat:

	Gans	Thibaut
German reception of Roman Law	9	14
Canon Law and Roman Law	11	12
Positive law	20	10, 8
Public and Private law	22	64
Written law	23	56
Edicts	24	32
Rescripts	25	32
Validity of law	28	24
Interpretation	31	42
Conflict of laws	34	35, 116
Repeal	36	37
Custom	37	15
Judicial custom or res judicata	38	16
Privilege	39	29
Legal persons	42	207
Physical life	43	228
Harm to reputation	45	240
Procedure	55	62

Like Thibaut, Gans was attracted to big, philosophically evocative, abstractions. But German legal academic thought was dogged by such categorizing, and Gans probably did not derive his specific categories directly from Thibaut. For example, both Gans and Thibaut distinguished prospective lawmaking from *jus respondendi* and associated the legal distinction with a more abstract dichotomy. But for Gans the regulative abstract dichotomy was between "law in the form of universality" (edicts, leges) and "law in the form of particularity" (rescripts).[148] Thibaut, too, associated prospective lawmaking (edicts) with "universal legal principles," and to these he counterposed rescripts, but he characterized the latter as "special" rather than particular.[149] For Thibaut these different kinds of Roman Law manifested an overarching dichotomy between universal and *special*, not particular; he reserved the term "particular" for a far narrower application to legal privilege and counterposed such particular law not to general law, but to *common* law.[150] In contrast, Gans associated privilege not with particularity but with "singularity."[151] Gans associated privilege with single law (*einzelne Gesetz*) and followed the Roman legal classification of privilege as *jus singulare*, as opposed to *jus commune*. But unlike Thibaut he did not associate *jus commune* with "common" (*gemeine*) laws. On the contrary, for Gans the law of singles as the negation of *jus commune* provided the transition to law in its subjective relation and his treatment of legal persons, which was part of his systematic treatment of common civil law.[152]

1.4.2. The "System" as Hegelian Science

Despite its fragmentary form as an outline, the *System of Roman Civil Law* was the most complete effort that Gans made at expressing his own field of legal study in the scientific form of a system. His ongoing work on the law of succession was a comparative treatment of a field of law in its development; consequently, his historical project never aimed at a comprehensive elaboration of any particular culture's legal system. Moreover, his project remained unfinished, so it never even achieved its more limited goal of surveying the evolution of the doctrines of succession law. Most of Gans's other writings were either polemical occasional pieces directed at narrow issues, or, like the Treatise appended to the *System*, they were critical treatments of methodological problems confronted in constructing a scientific and systematic treatment of law.

The project of making legal study scientific in the sense of organizing its subject matter into a comprehensive system derived explicitly from Hegel. And Gans understood his work in elaborating a system of Roman Law as a component part of the greater scientific project of working towards the all-embracing system that embodied Hegelian absolute knowledge. It is, perhaps, no coincidence that Gans conceived the project of the *System* and composed it during the summer of 1826 – coinciding with the height of his initial enthusiasm for the Hegelian Society for Scientific Criticism.

We have already observed how Gans in lectures on Hegel's philosophy of law treated law far more concretely than Hegel and significantly redefined the contents of the philosophy of law, emphasizing it as a systematic study of private law. Hegel's own published efforts at a system of legal philosophy, the *Encyclopedia* (1817) and *Philosophy of Right* (1821), had reduced law proper to such a small part of the system and treated the components of law in such vague terms that they offered Gans precious little guidance. Indeed, Gans's *System of Roman Law* could be considered the first Hegelian exposition of a system of legal doctrine.

Hegel's vagueness had stemmed from his theoretical focus on the interrelationship of basic ideas, rather than details. But Hegel's vagueness also manifested a real lack of interest in and ignorance of doctrinal law. Even in focusing on organization, however, Hegel did not succeed in constructing a framework for a system of law that could be completed by his followers. On the contrary, Hegel left a largely indeterminate scheme; and by building up from one view of the system, Gans effectively constructed an entirely new structure. Gans's creative reworking of Hegel was most apparent in those fields of law in which Gans had special interest. For example, Gans placed the system of the law of succession at the end of his system. This sequence was consistent with Hegel's treatment of succession in the transition from the Family to Civil Society. But Hegel's system hardly required this sequence. Indeed, Hegel's ambiguous references to the law of succession might equally have suggested separating the law of testate and intestate succession and treating testamentary transfers as part of legislation under civil society.[153]

Gans did not differ from Hegel only in his handling of individual components of the system. Rather there was a deeper systematic incongruity between Gans's and Hegel's basic approach. Though Gans sought in Hegel the means to make legal study scientific and systematic, Gans did not elaborate his system of law as part of an encyclopaedic exposition of scientific knowledge. His system's exact relation to Hegel's was not clear. As a system of Roman Law, understood as the law of the Romans, Gans's work constituted a contribution towards universal world history. But as a system of Roman Law, understood as a component of private civil law, Gans's work constituted part of the systematic treatment of law. History and law occupied two different places in Hegel's scheme and played two different functions in his philosophy. Gans never addressed the incongruity and may have been entirely unaware or indifferent to it.

For Gans the Hegelian promise of science and system translated above all into a guaranty of the absolute autonomy of academic legal study. Such study, like history, was a result of intellectual detachment and observation, which had empirical appeal: "A system of the science of law must necessarily begin with what law is." The subjective study led to a separation of law from its study – in a way that might be curiously reconciled politically through codification and philosophically through the systematic reintegration of the different components of the law.[154] Gans rejected the Historical School's reliance on historical research for political reasons, but he also warned that the reliance by academic legal study upon such research seriously threatened the integrity of law as an academic discipline. In accusing the Historical School of being "unphilosophical" and "unscientific" in this context, Gans invoked Hegelian science to enforce a rigorous autonomy of law. His distance from Hegel is evinced by the specific legal meaning he ascribed to the term *Aufhebung*. The term, usually translated "sublation," is a core part of Hegelian vocabulary, and for Hegel it denoted the simultaneous destruction and retention of some idea or thing. Gans, however, in attacking the Historical School, used the term in its narrower legal meaning of cancelling or repealing a statute, with the curiously non-Hegelian result that he protested against the Historical School's attempted *Aufhebung* of law.[155] By this Gans meant to protest the erosion of the disciplinary integrity of law that resulted from improper recourse to other disciplines like history. Conversely, he sought to redeem law as an autonomous academic discipline and to secure it from the eroding influences of romanticism by establishing it as a science and system. Gans approached law differently from Hegel. For Gans, making law philosophical and scientific meant separating it from other studies. For Hegel, a scientific treatment of law had meant ignoring law proper and focusing on those aspects of the study of law that related it to other parts of the system of science.

Gans also deviated from Hegel in his treatment of the components of law. The novelty of Gans's approach to law was obscured in part by the vagueness of Hegel's own treatment of law. It is questionable whether Gans deliberately set about to revise the Hegelian architectonic. In the few cases where Hegel provided a detailed scheme for classifying legal doctrines or institutions, Gans followed Hegel closely.[156] On the other hand, where Hegel did not provide a hierarchical framework for organizing material, Gans did not hesitate to erect one, even when doing so challenged Hegel's organizational assumptions.

Gans understood that Hegel's exclusion of delicts from the philosophy of law had been deliberate and had reflected Hegel's opinion that the category of delicts was inherently irrational. Hegel understood delicts or torts as the private recovery for a *wrong*, and he considered the core value supporting such a recovery to be retribution rather than compensation. Accordingly, for Hegel public or state authority was the only legitimate source for sanctions for wrongful conduct, and he reclassified delicts as a subpart of public law rather than private law. (Hegel believed his judgment was supported by the omission of separate category of delicts from the Prussian Civil Code.) Although Gans conceded that the category of delicts should not be included in a scientific treatment of modern private law, Gans retained the classification in his treatment of obligations (sections 268–84). He justified the classification by insisting on the importance of the category under Roman Law,[157] but Gans's reluctance to follow Hegel dogmatically into conflating delicts and public law probably also reflected Gans's legal training, which made him aware of the autonomy of delicts as a source of private rights – notwithstanding the fact that the category lacked rationality for Hegel.

Gans also creatively provided organization for a great bulk of material for which Hegel provided no clues. The scope of Gans's achievement is apparent from a comparison of corresponding material by Hegel.

Hegel	Gans
1. Abstract Law	1. Law in General
1. Property	2. Property Law
Possession	Possession
Use of the thing	Property
Alienation of property	[three chapters]
2. Contract	3. Law of Obligations
3. Wrong	
Unintentional wrong	Delicts
Deception	
Coercion and Crime	
2. Morality	
3. Order based on Custom	
1. Family	4. Family Law
Marriage	Marriage
Family wealth	
Childrearing	Paternal power
2. Civil Society	
System of needs	
Administration of justice	
Police and corporate power	
3. The State	
Constitutional Law	
International Law	
World History	
	5. Law of Succession
	[six chapters]

Most important, Gans changed the entire character of the system of law by collapsing Roman Law into what Hegel relegated to the first third of his philosophy of law, so-called "abstract formal law." This was consistent with Gans's treatment of Hegel's philosophy of law in his lectures after Hegel's death; there Gans interpreted Hegel's system as a framework for private law, and he employed only the first third of Hegel's *Elements of the Philosophy of Law* as the text for his course coverage.[158] Gans excluded any treatment of material that corresponded to the contents of Morality and Order based on Custom in Hegel's system.

While the sequence of Gans's coverage was influenced by Hegel, Gans rejected Hegel's tripartite organization. Instead he organized the system of Roman Law in five books. He treated the law of civil procedure in the first book, whereas Hegel had treated procedure under Order based on Custom. Gans included a separate treatment of delicts.

The most striking innovation was Gans's adoption of a whole new component of his system on the law of succession (Book Five). This had no counterpart in Hegel. Gans also departed from Hegel by concluding with a reconsideration of possession, a topic that Hegel had treated at the start in his system of law.

The departure of Gans from Hegel is still more clear if the actual structure and contents of Gans's system is compared to corresponding parts of Hegel's:

Gans	Hegel
1. Law in General	
1) Law in Objective Relation	
2) Law in Subjective Relation	
3) Realization of Law or On Legal Procedure	[Order based on Custom]
2. Property Law	Property
1) Physical Things	
2) Possession	1) Possession
3) Property	2) Use
4) Usufruct and Servitudes	3) Alienation
5) Liens	
6) Emphyteusis and Superficies	
3. Law of Obligations	2. Contract
1) Obligations in General	
2) Contracts and Similar Obligatory Relationships	
3) Delicts and related Obligatory Relationships	[3. Wrong]
4) On the Movement and Satisfaction of Obligations	
4. Family Law	[Ethical Life: part 1: Family]
1) Marriage	1) Marriage
2) Paternal Power and Kinship	2) Family wealth
3) Guardianship	3) Childrearing
5. Law Of Succession	[transition]
1) Concept of the Roman Law of Succession	
2) Relation of Testamentary succession to intestate succession	
3) The Testamentary System, or on Wills, Legacies, Entailed Estates, and Gifts causa mortis	
4) Intestate Succession	
5) Doctrine of Inheritance	
6) On bonorum possessio in Opposition to hereditas	

Hegel profoundly influenced Gans's method. This was evident in Gans's commitment to a system and science of law. Examples of Gans's adoption of specific doctrines from Hegel are pervasive and readily apparent to a reader familiar with Hegel. Hegel's influence was manifest in Gans's definition of law as the realization of freedom (section 19), his distinction between law (*Recht*) and positive law (*Gesetz*) (23), his treatment of the legal person as the subject of law (42), and in his idea of property as the external sphere of freedom (112).

Hegel's organizational emphasis on transitional and mediating categories, which was expressed formally in a preference for tripartite schemes, also influenced Gans's treatment of important topics.[159] Even when Hegel did not himself treat a legal relationship in his system, Gans often used general principles from Hegel to organize legal material. For instance, Gans organized treatment of paternal power (sections 326–36):

1. Origin of paternal power
   1. Immediate origin
   2. Mediated origin
   3. Unity of immediate and mediated origin
2. Legal relations of paternal power
3. Termination of paternal power

Gans occasionally invoked tripartite schemes that seemed motivated more by commitment to threefold forms than by the role the forms played in actually shaping the contents – though this formalism, too, found ample precedent in Hegel. For example, Gans classified the contents of the law of succession under a three-part scheme (sections 429–35.) Yet, despite language about mediation, it is difficult to see what was being mediated, or how the dichotomy was to be surmounted:

1. On the immediate relation of the heir to the inheritance
2. On the mediated relation of heirs to the inheritance
3. On the renunciation of inheritance

Gans's overt commitment to Hegel obscured his originality. By applying Hegel's principles to his own ends in the system of Roman Law, Gans effected significant modification of Hegel's method. Furthermore, Gans's adoption of Hegelian principles was incomplete. Notwithstanding his adoption of Hegelian mediating categories, his system retained an underlying preference for organizational bifurcation, which led to numerous dichotomizing definitions and classifications. Indeed, in places it looks like Gans simply inserted a Hegelian tripartite scheme on top of material that derived its organizational coherence from an underlying non-mediated definition or scheme. For instance, though Gans inserts a triadic classification into his chapter on property (section 116), that scheme covered only the methods of acquiring property. The contents of that chapter were actually organized according to the following distinctions (which were never mediated): property distinguished from possession (112); property divided into *dominium* (two kinds) and *bonae fidei possessio*. Indeed, two of the three components of the only triad comprised a most un-Hegelian dichotomy:

Methods of acquiring:

1. Immediate acquisition
    1) occupation (four sorts listed)
    2) accession
2. Acquisition mediated by change in the thing
    1) retention of the fabricated thing
    2) change into a different kind of thing
3. Acquisition mediated by another person

The dichotomizing method pervaded the next chapter, too, which was divided into Usufruct and Servitudes. Usufruct is defined as the separation of use from enjoyment (section 136), and servitudes are subdivided into two basic kinds (section 145).

Gans's incomplete adoption of Hegelian methodology was reflected in his peculiar use of Hegel's terminology. We noted earlier that Gans's criticized the Historical School for seeking the "cancellation" (*Aufhebung*) of law. There Gans employed Hegel's terminology in a derogatory fashion that was incompatible with Hegel's own distinctive use. Gans similarly employed the verb (*aufheben*) to denote a termination of legal relationships. He employed the term to denote the cancellation of marriage by legal annulment (section 320), the cancellation of family bonds by legal emancipation (section 338), and the cancellation of guardianship, not by completion or coming of age but by the resignation or wrongdoing of the guardian (section 360).

Like Hegel, Gans explicitly incorporated transitional material into his system. But whereas Hegel devoted such great attention to the transitions that they often overshadowed the components being related through the transitions, Gans gave scant independent role to the transitional material. Most often, Gans's transitions constituted mere sketches or suggestions devoid of content. No important topic of Roman Law was placed in any transition section.

On the other hand, Gans reworked the law of succession that Hegel relegated to transitional material linking discussions of the family and civil society. By erecting the law of succession into an autonomous component and the conclusion of his system, Gans established the legal integrity of the law of succession at the same time that he subtly but fundamentally redefined the science of law to be a system whose contents were drawn from private law.

1.5. INHERITANCE AND LAW

> Was du ererbt von deinen Vätern hast,
> Erwirb es, um es zu besitzen!
>
> Goethe[160]

Gans devoted the last book of his system to the law of succession. Counting the material on family law and guardianship, nearly one-fourth of his system was devoted to laws regulating the descent of property after death. This extended treatment of succession obviously reflected Gans's personal interests and expertise in the law of succession. And his interest in systematizing the law of succession led him to treat that material with particular care. It stands out as the most original part of his system.

Gans devoted much of his life work to research on the history of the law of succession. But he never completed his historical investigations, nor did he publish a systematic exposition of the law of succession. At his death the *System of Roman Civil Law* remained the only work in which he succeeded in giving any part of the law of succession the kind of coherent scientific form that his Hegelian principles demanded. The *System of Roman Civil Law* thus revealed the power of Gans's concern with the law of succession at the same time that it provided unique insight into Gans's theory of succession.

It is difficult to reconstruct the sources of Gans's interest in the law of succession. It is obvious that Gans gave much greater weight to the substantive law of succession than Hegel, but it is, perhaps, Hegel's neglect of the topic rather than Gans's preoccupation with it that requires an explanation. For Gans's extensive treatment of the substantive law of succession was characteristic of eighteenth-century legal theorists. The most relevant model for a systematic treatment of the law of the Digest, Thibaut's *System of the Law of the Pandects*, had devoted 182 out of the 300 sections in the "Law of Things" – about one-fifth of the total textual coverage of the work – to testate and intestate succession under Roman Law.

Gans's and Thibaut's concern with the law of succession is only partly explained by the expansive coverage of that law by the Digest itself. Contemporary German laws of succession certainly did not incorporate the detailed doctrines of Roman Law elaborated by Gans and Thibaut. Patterns of succession varied widely throughout the German-speaking jurisdictions, notwithstanding a supposedly common Roman common-law heritage. Even where Roman Law had influenced the codification of inheritance laws (as in Württemberg in 1555 and 1610), the results did not adopt the Digest in detail, nor did they tend towards interstate uniformity. German private law of succession remained a chaotic jumble of hundreds of competing systems and jurisdictions, with no uniform rules of decision. Political reality and the facts of life – justified, if it were necessary, by principles of private international law – tended to leave the legal disposition of both land and property to the legal jurisdiction best able to enforce its rule. This in turn placed extraordinary weight on the fact of possession. The concern of legal academicians with the problems of succession at death thus reflected a practical legal problem. But the academic concern with inheritance law also manifested a pervasive cultural phenomenon that was manifested throughout Europe.

1.5.1. Cultural Criticism of Inheritance Law

Concern by legal scholars in the eighteenth and early nineteenth century with the substantive law of succession mirrored a deepseated cultural preoccupation with inheritance and the more general problems of the passage of traits over time and the control of the present by preceding generations. To take one example (influenced by Gans), in Heine's *The Hartz Journey*, a character declares that no democracy can be achieved without reform of the laws of succession.[161]

The complexity of laws regulating inheritance, their effect in promoting the continued control of the present by the dead, and their association with social or political institutions identified with the medieval past – all converged to make the law of succession the natural focus for powerful intellectual and emotional enmity. Yet the very reasons that caused thinkers since the Enlightenment to view succession laws as politically odious and conceptually irrational served to render the law of succession most deeply resistant to reform.

These general sources of concern with succession throughout Europe were compounded in central Europe by a legal crisis in the law of succession. It is anachronistic to think there were any coherent rules of general application that regulated succession throughout the German states. The actual disposition of property at death was the result of hundreds of factors, including the place of death, the location of property, and the first to take possession. The secular authority did not exercise undisputed control over succession, and even if it did, the proliferation of legislative and customary sources of secular law combined with complicated layers, sources, and varieties of personal tenure to make patterns of succession baffling, and the application of rules unpredictable from case to case. Drafting, settling, and administering of estates was one of the most esoteric parts of legal practice throughout Europe. In England Blackstone's lectures brought some order to the structure of estates and tenures and revealed the mysteries behind the family settlement to the university educated gentry. In France the Code made the law of succession accessible to the literate population. In German states, however, no such coherent elaboration of laws regulating succession was possible. To this day no single work dares attempt an exposition of nineteenth-century laws of succession in the German states.

Given the esoteric nature of academic legal scholarship, it is uncertain whether legal academic authorities understood actual laws of succession. The law professorate certainly made no effort to teach such laws, which (to the extent they could have been determined with any precision) were subject to change every few miles. The absence of clear rules of general application would predictably have left the succession of property subject to abuse by local authorities, but the evidence is unclear. Alternative institutions and professional authorities may have filled gaps in the way that ad hoc practices in England effectively provided for extrajudicial testamentary transfers long before to the Statute of Wills.

Estate law was unique in that most middle class Germans unavoidably suffered some personal contact during their lives with the administration of the law of succession. The variety of such experiences and the lack of sources makes it difficult to reconstruct them, though literary sources confirm widespread contemporary concern – and dissatisfaction – with laws of succession. Authors assumed critical attitudes on the part of their readers towards existing laws of succession.

1.5.2. Rationalizing the Law of Succession

Achieving a uniform, coherent law of succession loomed as one of the greatest theoretical challenges for rationalist legal theory in the nineteenth-century German-speaking world. The academic concern with technical and esoteric issues of the law of succession was motivated and shaped by attitudes with deep roots in the culture.

For Gans, as for Thibaut, Roman Law provided a model for a coherent and rational law of succession. Both scholars embraced Roman Law as a constituent of the common civil law and as a source for rationalizing the rules of succession throughout the German state. And both, in rationalizing and systematizing the complicated Roman Law rules of succession, demonstrated the feasibility of articulating and codifying a civil law of succession for the German states. Roman Law was simultaneously a source of the law of succession and a model for its reform.

But Thibaut and Gans placed quite different emphasis on the goals of succession in their respective systematic treatments of Roman Law. Thibaut was more concerned to enhance the rational administration of the laws by offering Roman Law as a valid source of uniform, coherent, and accessible legal authority. He was far more concerned than Gans with elaborating Roman Law doctrines of succession, and he accordingly followed the contents and form of the Digest more closely than Gans. Thibaut retained many of the categories and distinctions found in Justinian, and in order to make his descriptive presentation of Roman Law more rational, Thibaut imposed a new, higher level of organization on top of the classification of doctrines present in the Digest. The result was a complicated hierarchy that succeeded in comprehending much of the material from Justinian but that related the contents externally, accidentally, and repetitiously. Some of the organizational weaknesses of Thibaut's treatment were evident from a selective reproduction of his scheme for the law of succession. (His various numbering systems for different levels are all converted to arabic numbers):

Thibaut's Treatment of Succession

2. Private Law
    1. The Law of Things
    ...
    2. Rights connected to things
        ...
        2. Things whose object is a *universitas*
           Introduction
            1. Inheritance
                1. Contract of inheritance
                2. Intestate succession
                3. Testamentary succession
                   [Testament, Substitution]
                   ...
                    2. Legacy and Testamentary Trusts
                        1. Legacy and Trust
                        2. Universal Trust
                        3. Common Principles of legacy and trust
                    3. Common Principles of Inheritance,
                       Legacy, and Testamentary trust
                       ...
                        3. Invalidity of testamentary
                           instruments

By retaining the Roman legal category of *universitas*, Thibaut subordinated the substance of the law of succession to lower categories, thus devaluing the importance of the concrete legal doctrines while inflating the importance of the abstraction under which they were elaborated. By preserving the Roman legal distinctions among legacies, trusts, testaments, and wills, Thibaut treated different methods of testamentary transfer in different places which corresponded to different levels of the system. Testamentary succession, comprising succession by testament and substitution, was treated as a subcategory of *Delation*. But legacies and testamentary trusts were treated later, after a section on the entry into inheritance, and those methods of testate succession were given systematic status equal to *Delation* rather than testaments and substitutions. The inadequacy of the organization for treating all of Thibaut's methodological concerns required the addition of components on "Common Principles of Legacy and Testamentary Trusts" and, at a different level of the hierarchy, "Common Principles of Inheritance, Legacy, and Testamentary Trusts."

In striking contrast, Gans valued Roman Law as a model for law reform more than as a source of uniform laws. Classical Roman Law had retained the core principle of universal succession. The appointment of an heir was the central validating event in any testamentary transfer, and the heir was substituted for the deceased in most legal relationships. The civil law thus came to view legacies as subtractions from the estate that passed to an heir. At a relatively late period Roman Law limited certain testamentary dispositions in order to protect the expectation of family members (who generally had a right to one-fourth of their intestate share). The primitive origins of the civil law rules of succession were reflected in the controlling power of formal requirements. The civil law ultimately recognized several forms of universal succession and at least four types of legacies.[162] The rights recognized by the civil law of succession were enforceable through a variety of actions (each regulated by its own formal peculiarities), but all were prosecuted in courts of ordinary procedure. At the same time, in a historical process frequently compared to the evolution of Equity in English law, the praetors provided supplemental remedies that expanded and modified the rules of succession.[163] Moreover, like the uses or trusts recognized at Equity, the praetorian trust-like rights imposed personal obligations which were enforceable in a separate judicial system, which offered some major advantages to parties seeking to enforce the trust-like interests.[164] Gaius (whom Gans studied intensively at Heidelberg) explicated the origins of the parallel systems of succession under the Roman Law. By the time of Justinian, the complexity of rules under each system, and the means for reconciling the two systems, had become formidable indeed.

Much of the Digest is devoted to explaining the myriad rules of succession. But under Justinian the two systems were ultimately consolidated. Gans no doubt saw the chaos of contemporaneous German private law mirrored in the Byzantine accumulation of ancient rules of succession. And in the fusion of rules under Justinian, he would have seen the promise of law reform under a code. Gans was far less concerned than Thibaut with absorbing and comprehensively describing the coverage of doctrines than with refashioning the content of the law of succession into a coherent body of law. Gans's reorganization and selective omission of materials from the Digest demonstrated that he was less concerned with providing a system that comprehended all of the substantive law of succession from Justinian than he was concerned to utilize materials from the Digest as contents for a coherent elaboration of the law that integrated those materials as part of a coherent, systematic overview of the body of law regulating succession.

Gans related the law of succession to other parts of Roman private law that effected the disposition of property rights at death. This led, as we have already seen, to altering the place of the law of succession in his system. By making the law of succession a separate part of the system, and by relocating it next to family law, Gans effectively established the law of succession as a coherent body of doctrinal law. He also reworked the internal organization of the law of succession so as to enhance its internal coherence. The background model for his system was the Hegelian idea of systematic science as a system of systems. Thus Gans designated the subchapter on the law of testamentary succession, which treated materials that were especially disorganized under Justinian, as the "Testamentary *System.*" Gans achieved far greater overall simplicity than Thibaut by removing superior layers from the architectonic and by placing subordinate layers containing substantive doctrines on the same level. Unlike Thibaut, Gans treated testate succession before intestate succession, and Gans assembled all the main methods of testamentary transfer and treated them together as part of the testamentary system.

Gans's System of Succession

V. The Law of Succession
   1. Concept of the Roman Law of Succession
   2. Relation of Testate and Intestate Succession
   3. Testamentary System (testaments, substitutions, legacies, trusts)
   4. Intestate Succession
   5. Doctrine of Inheritance (*hereditas*)
   6. *Bonorum possessio* in Opposition to Inheritance

This novel arrangement derived from neither Thibaut nor Hegel but rather expanded a schema that Gans had first employed in 1820 in his commentary on Gaius.[165] This organization manifested Gans's underlying goal of comprehending all methods for transferring legal interests at death within this system. This was a revolutionary approach to the law of succession. For example, Gans treated gifts causa mortis – gifts made during life that are contingent upon the donor dying – as part of the testamentary succession. Thibaut had treated such transfers as part of the general treatment of gifts in an entirely different part of his system.[166]

Equally important was Gans's rejection of the proliferation of testamentary techniques in favor of an overall dichotomy of transfers into testate and intestate succession. "The Roman law of succession is thus subdivided essentially into intestate succession on one side and into testamentary succession on the other side." (Section 366.) This simple classification appears natural only in hindsight; through it Gans discarded an organization that was subservient to the confusing, overlapping techniques that were recognized by diverse sources of legal authority over the course of centuries of Roman legal development. Instead, his dichotomy assumed a rational distinction that subtended all such transfer methods. In one group Gans placed devices through which individuals exercised their will – "[a]bstract freedom of choice" (section 386) – to control transfers after death. In the other group Gans placed the doctrines that controlled transfer after death in the absence of an effective exercise of individual testamentary control.

The idea of succession behind Gans's organization emphasized testamentary transfer as the norm. Indeed, in his lectures on the philosophy of law, Gans cited Roman Law's recognition of testamentary transfers as one of its chief superiorities over German law.[167] Intestate succession, treated second, appeared as a sort of system of default rules. Gans's sequential treatment of testate and intestate succession reflected more naturally the legal approach to estate planning or the legal analysis of property interests that result from death, but this treatment deviated from that of Justinian, Thibaut, Hegel, and the French Civil Code. What is more, Gans's overall sequence reversed the historical order in which he placed the emergence of such doctrines.[168]

The theoretical amalgamation of praetorian and civil law rules of succession under Justinian provided Gans with a model for consolidating different regional laws of succession at the same time that it provided a model for a mixed system of testate and intestate succession. Gans did not promote a legal system that authorized unlimited testamentary control; rather he promoted a modern system of rules of succession that authorized limited testamentary control, but which preferred the testamentary disposition of property properly within a testator's power. The important political implications of Gans's system appeared in his exclusion of administrative ad hoc decisionmaking and judicial discretion in the application of the rules.

It goes without saying that Gans's System of Roman Law propounded a construction of Roman legal practice that comported with his own legal values. His tendentious use of Roman Law affected his treatment of sources and even rendered his commentary unreliable in places. To take one example, his commitment to a mixed system of succession was difficult to reconcile with the Roman Law principle that one cannot die partly testate and partly intestate, so he sought to qualify the Roman Law principle against partial intestacy. To this end, he emphasized that a "variety of opinions" (section 364) could be attributed to the jurists on the meaning of the prohibition. His authority involved Cicero for the only time in the work, and he added citations to soldiers' wills and other special cases.[169] His treatment of sources thus supported his overarching view of the law of succession as two independent systems of testate and intestate succession and of "the union of both in compulsory right of succession" (section 367).

1.6. The System as Polemic

Imagine no possession.
I wonder if you can.

John Lennon

Savigny had begun his important treatise on the law of succession with the observation that the law of possession developed out of the "fact" of possession.[170] Gans spent much of his career attacking the view that possessory rights devolved historically out of possessory relationships. Gans brought a passion, bordering on monomania, to his attack on Savigny's theory of possession that has baffled scholars.[171] At the end of his life, Gans identified his theoretical struggle against the Historical School as one of the three main achievements of his life.[172]

Gans's passion was fueled in part by his personal loathing of Savigny's reactionary politics and anti-Semitism. Savigny's campaign to prevent Gans's appointment to the law faculty in 1826 was fresh in mind when Gans composed his *System of Roman Civil Law*.[173] Polemical considerations affected the organization and contents of the system, and Gans set forth his argument in considerable detail in the accompanying Treatise. While pretending to admire Savigny's book on possession,[174] Gans proceeded to criticize it for failing to treat the status or meaning of the concept of possession. Gans's most fundamental grievance, however, was that Savigny's effort to trace the law of possession from the "fact" of possessory relationships confused natural and legal "fact." Gans objected that Savigny wrongly based a right (possession) on a wrong (wrongful dispossession).

> In this lies the weakness of Savigny's method of development. A wrong is obviously first possible in general when a [recognized] right precedes it: a right can never be based on a wrong, for wrong is merely the negation of [the] right and thus contains the positive expression of the right.[175]

Gans continued the argument for five more printed pages.

Twelve years later, Gans devoted an entire polemical tract, his last published work, to reiterating his argument. "Possession thus entails right and is not merely a natural condition which is not simultaneously also a legal relationship."[176] Even though Savigny had conceded that mere physical possession imparted no right so that dispossession entailed no legal injury, Gans protested that Savigny still did not embrace the true doctrine that possession could never derive from legal prohibitions of wrongful takings but was instead a species of property.[177]

Gans regularly attacked Savigny's view of possession in his lectures on the philosophy of law, and his attacks became increasingly bitter over the years.[178] It is clear from the outline for the System of Roman Law that Gans meant to employ his lectures on the Digest to polemicize against Savigny's view of possession. Thus the System began (section 2) with a critical reference to the scholarship of the Historical School.[179] His systematic typology of Roman Law expressed a strong preference for law (*Recht*) in the "universal form of legislation (*Gesetz*)" over the merely incipient forms of custom (sections 23–24) and this constituted an implicit criticism of the values of the Historical School and supported pro-Code politics.[180]

In his system he took special pains to refute Savigny's wrongheaded view of possession as a "fact." First, Gans relegated purely factual relationships to natural science, not law. (Section 92.) Second, he began his treatment of possession by referring to the variety of views on the subject and repudiating Savigny's view: "Possession is no mere factum, and it does not arise as *law* by the circuitous path of *injustice*." (103) Gans returned to attack Savigny's doctrine of possession at the very end of the system. Only the polemical aims of his system explain why he treated *bonorum possessio* separately at the end of the law of succession. *Bonorum possessio* was a right of universal succession that the praetor developed that paralleled the inheritance (*hereditas*) recognized by the civil law.[181] In some cases the praetorian rules led to different results, and the alternative praetorian law offered significant procedural advantages, so that it ultimately displaced the rules of the civil law.[182] The two systems were effectively merged under Justinian.[183]

The historical course of *bonorum possessio* offered striking support for Gans's basic argument against Savigny that possession presupposed property rights and was not a mere exercise of dominion over a thing. For the praetor initially establishes *bonorum possessio* as a sort of right of possession that supplemented the inheritance: the legal right was clearly the result of the act of the sovereign, not a "fact" of possession. Moreover, the complex legal incidents of such possessory rights evolved into a complex law of succession that actually altered the substantive Roman Law of inheritance.[184] Thus in ending with *bonorum possessio*, Gans ended his lectures, as he had begun them, with an attack on Savigny's core theory that possession derived from the fact of control or custody over a thing.

At issue in Gans's polemic against Savigny was the source and nature of property rights. Legal theorists throughout Europe expressed concern with the ultimate source of property rights; this was the legal expression of ongoing exploration and debate about the sources of law and the nature of civil society. A remarkably similar (but unrelated) debate took place in English legal scholarship. Blackstone had observed in 1765 that possession or occupancy established the right of the possessor to the thing possessed, unless there were a better legal claim; and he suggested that social laws arose to assure continuous or permanent property.[185] Though Blackstone's general theory of the origins of property law was not directly relevant to any of his observations about specific English laws, the passage provoked prolonged controversy among the annotators to Blackstone. Edward Christian, for example, sought to root the rights of possession, and even the rights of succession, in natural law.[186] Wooddeson and Ryland, on the other hand, emphasized the roots of property rights in social convention.[187] This debate was not just about the nature of the right to possession; rather it concerned the source of law generally.[188] The debate that transpired in footnotes and revisions to Blackstone was fueled by underlying differences about the power of the legislature to interfere with and to regulate property rights. It also revealed differences about the proper role of natural rights argument in accounting for the content of English law.

Debate about root claims of right reflected broader cultural concerns about inheritance and possession. Goethe's "Catechization" evidenced this broad interest while illuminating the underlying links between the cultural concerns with possession and inheritance:

> Teacher: Consider, child! from whom do these gifts come? You can have nothing from yourself.
> Child: Oh, I get it all from Daddy.
> Teacher: And he? where did he get it from?
> Child: From Grandpapa.
> Teacher: No, no! How did it all come to Grandpapa then?
> Child: He took it.[189]

Gans promoted the social-convention position that Blackstone had advocated. By criticizing the idea that legal rights of possession evolved out of actual possession, Gans repudiated the effort to derive legal rights from relationships that were purely natural. But Gans's argument was not deontological. On the contrary, Gans rejected the idea of separating social relationships like possession from the application of overarching and universal rules of law. Thus he argued that a taking could never be considered *wrongful* unless the person dispossessed were considered to have a right, howsoever incipient, to continued possession. The idea of the wrong – which might legally support a right of revenge, retribution, or compensation – could not exist conceptually independent of the idea of "right."

For Gans, the effort to explain the genesis of right out of wrong was necessarily circular and futile. But this circularity did not demonstrate the relativity or subjectivity of law; it manifested rather the inescapable presence of the legal dimension in any discussion of human relations. It was not that property could not be derived historically from tort or crime; rather tort remedies and criminal sanctions presupposed the existence of legal rights that made the wrongful violation subject to legal remedy. Gans thus rejected natural law as a genetic explanation but elevated it to an omnipresent feature of social behavior. As such, his theory comported with basic values and doctrines of Hegel's philosophy. Natural law provided an absolute, irreducible foundation for human laws.

It is difficult to understand the fervor that Gans brought to his attack on Savigny's doctrine.[190] The theoretical status of possessory rights and law in general may have had relevance to general metaphysical beliefs, but Gans did not engage in polemics against philosophical opponents whose views were far more antagonistic to the tenets of Hegelian idealism than Savigny. The debate about the status of possessory rights had little direct application to any pressing legal issue. But the debate had important indirect consequences for the property rights and concomitant constitutional powers exercised by feudal lords throughout Central Europe. In fact, Savigny's Treatise on Possession was a direct reaction to an work that Thibaut had published the previous year. Thibaut had denied that the Roman Law of possession supported the feudal lords' claims to their demesnes by right of acquisitive prescription.[191] Savigny rejected Thibaut's argument and attempted to show how the fundamental principle of the Roman Law of possession, as modified on German soil, established a legal and constitutional foundation for the property rights and constitutional power seized by the feudal lords.[192]

Savigny's treatise shunned direct political discussion; it was "a model of unpolitical political writing,"[193] and offered few points for direct political attack. Gans's critique of Savigny's views of possession employed abstract language borrowed from Hegel, and Gans pursued Savigny with a persistence and passion that looks ridiculous today. Nevertheless, the controversy reflected a contemporaneous crisis in *private* law throughout the German states that has been largely ignored – notwithstanding an extensive body of literature on the inherently weak treatment of rights in the *public* law of the period.[194] Key to understanding the debate is appreciating the way in which Savigny's extraordinary scholarship, by rooting possession in unarticulated custom and tradition, and by valuing the historical evidence of custom and tradition as authority, powerfully promoted, vindicated, and legitimized possession as the basis for claims of right to property.

Validating possession was not just a historical rationalization for the power of feudal lords; rooting property in possession constituted an implicit justification for weak and ineffective legal authority. The failure of legal institutions throughout the German states effectively to resolve private disputes necessarily placed a premium upon the "fact" of possession. Savigny's doctrine thus projected into history the contemporary political and legal reality; at the same time, his doctrine served to glorify the weakness of legal institutions that characterized the legal status quo. In 1811 Goethe recalled the Imperial Chamber's inability to impose constitutional order; he expressed with irony the age's devaluation of private law and identified the extreme importance of possession that resulted from the failure of courts to enforce private law remedies.

> [M]atters of weightier import, the lawsuits properly so called, remained behindhand; and this was no misfortune. The only concern of the state is, that possession shall be certain and secure: whether it is also legal, is of less consequence. Hence, from the monstrous and ever-swelling number of delayed suits, no mischief arose to the empire. Against people who employed force, provision was already made, and with such matters could be settled: but those, on the other hand, who legally disputed about possession, lived, enjoyed, or starved, as they could; they died, were ruined, or made it up; but all this was the good or evil of individual families. . .[195]

Savigny's historical treatment of possession comported perfectly with the diffused, weak, and ineffective systems of private law throughout the German states that relied principally on possession, administered through *public* law sanctions for forceful, wrongful dispossession. The association of delicts and wrongs with the enforcement of possessory rights probably explains why Gans so eagerly followed Hegel (and the Prussian Code) in eliminating delicts, as part of the law of obligations, from private law.[196]

For Gans a chief virtue of a code was its firm justification of possession by rooting actual possession in legal property rights. It was no accident that his commentaries on Prussian legislative reform in 1830 commenced with a treatment of the rights of finders and "On Unjustified Possession."[197]

The force of Gans's attack on Savigny's doctrine of possession was thus a measure of the force of his revulsion against contemporaneous private law. But the failure of his views to achieve greater currency was not only the result of the political dominance of existing legal institutions and the academic dominance achieved by the Historical School. Of course, Gans's failure may also reflect internal problems in his theory. His own doctrine confused normative and a descriptive arguments. On the one hand, he argued descriptively that the existing priority accorded possession (bad as it was) necessarily embodied a system of private rights. On the other hand, he argued normatively that possessory rights should be rooted in fixed property rights, published preferably in the form of a code. But in the end he offered no bridge between his criticism of the present and his program for the future. And the priority that he accorded to legislation relegated the solution of the crisis of private law to those political forces whose indifference to private law had led to the crisis.

When Germany emerged as a unified state in the late nineteenth century, it lacked the firm, rationally articulated common private law rights that Gans had insisted were necessary for law. A common culture of private law rights was provided not by the gradual expansion of rules of uniform application but, on the one hand, by competing academic theories of common native German laws, and, on the other hand, by ubiquitous (but inefficacious) doctrines of Roman Law associated with pervasive principles of reason. The civil code adopted in 1897 was imposed on top of a social and legal culture that, as a result, never fully internalized the values of private law rights or integrated them into a national political identity that resisted their external manipulation by political authority.

CHAPTER 2

GANS'S *SYSTEM OF ROMAN CIVIL LAW IN OUTLINE* (1827)

Translator's Note

The *System of Roman Civil Law*, translated here for the first time, was the first half of a larger book, *System of Roman Civil Law in Outline with a Treatise on the Study and System of Roman Law* (1827).[198] This system constituted Gans's only effort to give a field of law the scientific form that his philosophical principles demanded.

Gans composed the book rapidly during the summer of 1826. The first half of the book, the system proper, was a law textbook devised for the use of students in his lectures on Roman Law, which he offered at the University of Berlin starting with his second term of teaching.[199] He offered the course (entitled *Pandekten*) in Winter 1826–27, Summer 1827, Summer 1828, Summer 1829, and Summer 1830.[200]

The publication of systematic works in such an outline or syllabus form had become commonplace throughout Europe by the nineteenth century. Hegel had published his Encyclopedia in the form of outlines for lectures, and Hegel's *Elements of the Philosophy of Law in Outline* had also appeared in that format. Gans's textbook was unusual, however, in that it combined the syllabus form with a parallel text of extensive annotations that both cited authority for the contents of his system and generously quoted the authority. His system thus provided students with a handy and affordable anthology of texts from the Digest.

The second half of Gans's book bore a separate title page, *On the Study and System of Roman Law*, but was paginated continuously with the first part.[201] This treatise was designed as commentary on the system that preceded it. The two parts of the book played distinct roles and addressed different audiences. The treatise engaged in polemic against various academic opponents, notably Savigny and the Historical School. While comprising a reflective discussion of the goals of the system, and while attempting to justify some of the system's organization, the critical discussion remained extraneous to the system; the treatise was not designed as part of the textbook for use of students, nor was it part of the systematic or scientific expression of Roman civil law. Gans did not derive from Hegel the practice of spatially distinguishing systematic and polemical texts, but there was ample contemporaneous authority for such a practice – for example in Goethe's organization of his *Theory of Colors*.

Omissions

The present translation omits the treatise. The treatise was not part of Gans's system proper, and I have discussed passages in the treatise that illuminate the system in Chapter 1. For the most part, the treatise's long, repetitious, and tendentious arguments would be of interest today only to students of the criticism of the Historical School. The treatise adds little to an understanding of the system. Moreover, unlike the system itself, the accompanying treatise has been reprinted and is easily accessible.[202]

This translation also omits Gans's extensive quotations from Roman Law authorities that were included in the footnotes to the system, but it preserves all of Gans's citations to those authorities. Because the quotations constituted over two-thirds of the original text of the system, their omission significantly reduces the size of the work. This excision of the quotations seemed desirable for several reasons in addition to brevity and economy. First, the actual text of the quotations in Gans's notes can be easily determined from the citations (which have been edited, corrected, and amplified so as to cite accurately the text passages that Gans had originally quoted). Second, printing the original quotations in Latin would have been superfluous, because readers interested in the Latin texts quoted by Gans would demand more reliable sources; on the other hand, readers seeking English translations can find better ones elsewhere than could possibly have been provided in these annotations.[203]

Because Gans's quotations are omitted, a general observation on the accuracy of his citations and quotations is necessary. Gans's Latin quotations were so accurate that there would be little point in identifying the inevitable printer's errors that were discovered. In contrast, his citations for the quotations were riddled with errors, both as regards the references and as regards the jurists to whom the quoted passages were attributed.[204] The accuracy of the Latin and the inaccuracy of the citations suggests that Gans provided the printer with a clean copy of the text of the Latin sources but provided handwritten citations (which were more easily misread by the printer). Some of the sorts of errors that appeared repeatedly support this inference. But while the errors may shed light on the process of composition and printing,[205] they can be ascribed to Gans as author only to the extent that he did not correct them in proofreading the text. Assuming that Gans proofread but did not verify the references, then the errors also support the conclusion, which is hardly surprising, that Gans did not know the Digest intimately enough to recognize numerous citation errors. In any event, this translation corrects all the citation errors without identifying them. (Scholars can easily locate the errors by comparing the citations provided by this translation with those in the original.) When Gans's notes improperly attributed juristic authority, however, his original attributions are retained and the correct authority is inserted [in brackets]. One Latin quotation in a note is included in this translation because Gans provided no citation, and I could not discover its source.

Terminology

Gans's German legal prose presents special challenges to translation when he employs Latin terms. Latin terms that are treated as foreign by Gans are not translated. A selective Glossary of Roman Law terms is appended. When a Latin term is adopted as vernacular or naturalized as a German legal term of art, I have tried to find an adequate English correlate. The difficulty in finding appropriate correlates for Roman Law ideas is aggravated by the difficulty of expressing the extent to which Roman Law terms were naturalized in contemporary German legal prose. It is often not clear whether a Latin term was adopted as part of the vernacular, whether the term was a legal term of art, or whether the term was used to refer to a historical concept or doctrine that was foreign to German law and language. The relationship of early nineteenth-century German legal theory to Roman Law (and especially Gans's own views on the close relationship of the two) prevents a clear differentiation. Capitalizations of substantives sometimes offer a clue, as for Querel in section 375, but Gans was not consistent. Thus it is not clear when terms like dolus (intent) or Mensor in section 283, are meant vernacularly.

I have tried, in accordance with contemporary translation conventions, to render terms faithfully and consistently by terminological correlates; and I have tried to render different German terms by different English ones. Nevertheless, Gans (like all writers) occasionally used different terms to mean the *same* thing, and that same thing can sometimes be best rendered by a single English word.[206] A special problem is presented by the terms *Recht* and *Gesetz*, which denote different types of law and which have different connotations. *Recht* (especially in the plural) can mean right in the sense of legal entitlement, but it is often used more generally to refer to law and justice. (Thus Philosophy of Law is *Rechtsphilosophie*.) *Gesetz* refers to a more specific kind of prescriptive rule, and it denotes written or positive laws. (Thus a code or compilation of laws is *Gesetzbuch*.) Laws of nature, however, are also denoted by *Gesetz*. It has been common to preserve the distinction between *Recht* and *Gesetz* in English translations of German philosophical prose (but not German legal prose). The translation of *Recht* invariably as "Right" and *Gesetz* as "law" has the merit of indicating the German term being translated; unfortunately, the resulting English prose is inaccurate (since there is simply no English term for "Right"), and it fails to communicate the vernacular or legal character of the German text. I have, accordingly, translated both terms as "law" on occasion; and in one passage where it is important to distinguish the two, *Gesetz* (denoting statutory law) is rendered as "[positive] law."

I translate *Sittlichkeit* as "order based on custom." Gans derived the term from Hegel, and like Hegel Gans meant to distinguish custom from both law and morality. Although order based on custom is often translated as the "ethical order," this confuses custom with morality. Both Hegel and Gans distinguished the non-coercive order of custom from the commands of morality (which was identified with the inner moral law of Kant). Moreover, "ethical order" implies a subjective standard of conduct that is almost the exact opposite of what Hegel and Gans meant. The closest English equivalent of the German is the antiquated nineteenth-century use of "manners" to designate the important norms of customary group behavior.[207] But the sources of the norms in custom (*Sitte*) are expressed even more strongly in the German.

A different problem arises where distinct German or Latin terms denote distinct institutions or doctrines that have no counterpart in Anglo-American jurisprudence. For example, Gans employed a variety of terms to describe different sorts of property interests, different sorts of guardianship relationships, and different sorts of testamentary (and nontestamentary) methods and instruments that have correlates in neither vernacular English nor Anglo-American legal terminology. The present translation necessarily makes some unsatisfactory compromises. In general, where a vernacular German term was employed, or where a Latin term was vernacularized, I have given priority to finding an English term (even when the English correlate is imperfect). The variety of German and Latin kinds of property in particular, are translated – albeit imperfectly – where possible. In one area, I have conceded defeat altogether, and I use the term guardian generally for *Vormundschaft*, *Tutel*, and *Cura* (with the original terms inserted in parentheses). In a few cases where my translation adopts a neologism or constitutes a guess, I have also included the original (in parentheses). This invariably reduces the *legal* accuracy of the translation but serves, I hope, to enhance its accessibility to scholars who have the sort of historical and philosophical interests that would lead them to look at the work of Gans.[208]

A special problem in translating foreign legal terminology into English arises from the dichotomy in English between the common use of many terms and the distinct legal use of the same terms. For example, the terms heir and inheritance are used in common English to denote all sorts of transfers of property at death, but the terms have a narrower legal meaning in English law as the descent at death of certain kinds of property interests in land where the dead person left no will. This translation places a premium on using English terminology with legal accuracy. Thus "succession" is generally preferred to "inheritance," though this detracts from readability and also fails to communicate the vernacular quality of the original.

Editorial amplifications are placed [in brackets]. Gans's original numbered footnote numbers are preserved and his notes are printed as footnotes (albeit abridged and edited) to distinguish them from my endnotes. *Italics* indicate Gans's use of both German euphatic type and italic type. Latin terms printed in roman in the original are not italicized here either.

Preface

The Treatise appended at the end of the Outline has so many of the basic features of a Preface that an actual Preface, so titled, seems unnecessary. This Preface will limit itself to explaining why the Treatise, which might be considered a waste of time, has been appended to the Outline. Since the outline is being disseminated to the general public, I thought that it should not be released without a scientific guide and advocate. The Treatise seeks in part to demonstrate that the arrangement of the system is not arbitrary, and it seeks in part to justify the work of pure classification of the theory of law, for such pure classification has understandably fallen into disrepute and has become virtually notorious. If an even more adequate scientific form were demanded for the Treatise, namely that the grounds of the work be contained in the work itself, then the dichotomy of the content and its supporting argument might be justified by the external goal of the outline as a supplement for lectures.

Nothing would please me more than to have a critic, who is both informed and exacting, to take the role of instructor and prove the inadequacy of this work. After such criticism I would gladly make corrections, and lectures offer the best opportunity for doing so. I will ignore purely subjective fault-finding.

Berlin, August 18, 1827.
Eduard Gans.

Introduction

1. Content and object of common civil law.

2. Methods of Treatment. Exegetic method. Dogmatic Method. Systematic Method. The Historical School.

3. The contemporary significance of common civil law. Its place in philosophy of law, history of law, practical law.

4. Roman law is reflected in the system of contemporary law. Conflict of principles of Roman Law and others. Agreement of the two, or Roman Law as source of private law in general.

5. External sources of information. On the components of common civil law.

6. Roman Law.
   A. Law before Justinian.
   B. Justinian law.
   C. Law after Justinian.

7. Pandects. Institutes. Codex. Novels.

8. Relation of these parts of the Justinian Compilation. Corpus juris civilis.

9. Reception of Roman Law in Germany. Its necessity. Its legal force. How it compares with Roman Law in other countries.

10. Editions of the corpus juris and the particular parts of the law. Literary observations. Forms of citation. Research aids.

11. Canon Law, as private law and not as church law.

12. Decretum Gratiani. Decrees of Gregory IX. Liber sextus. Clementine. Corpus juris canonici clausum. Other parts of Canon Law. Relation of the parts.

13. Editions. Research aids. Literary observations.

[14.] Relationship of Canon and Roman Law.

15. Imperial laws.

16. Relation to the provincial laws. Relations to Roman and Canon Law.

17. Research aids with regards to the common civil law. Textbooks and other kinds of writings.

18. Overview of the system.

First Book: On Law in General

First Chapter: On Law in Objective Relation

19. On law as the realization of freedom. Roman ways of thinking and definitions.[1] Multiple meanings of the word jus.

20. Law as positive law. Relation to natural law – jus naturale, gentium, civile.[2]

21. From which Roman Law is properly distinguished – jus vile, honorarium.[3] How far this is only a Roman distinction.

22. Law as public law and private law.[4] Significance of this division for Roman Law.

23. Law (*Recht*) defines itself as something externally given, posited, [positive] law (*Gesetz*), jus scriptum. Or it remains merely in its ground [as] jus non scriptum, custom.

24. On jus scriptum. What it includes.[5] On [positive] law in the form of universality.[6] Edicts, leges edictales, particular laws. On the difference between mandate, decree, interlocutiones, sanctiones v. jussiones pragmaticae.

25. On law in the form of particularity. Rescripts.[7]

26. On law as legislation – constitutiones. Division of these.

27. On the contemporary distinction of laws. What significance Roman designations retain today.

28. Binding force of laws when promulgated. Publication. Measure of validity for different kinds of laws. Division of laws according to the criterion of validity.

29. Laws are not valid before promulgation. On the retroactive force of laws.

30. On those subjected to laws.[8]

31. On the agreement of content and form or expression of laws. On the separation of the two. On the reintegration or interpretation. Different kinds of interpretation as regards their source of explanation and as regards their method of research and goal.[9]

---

[1] Dig. Just. 1.1.1.pr (Ulpian); Dig. Just. 1.1.1.1 (Ulpian); Dig. Just. 1.1.10.1–2 (Ulpian).

[2] Dig. Just. 1.1.1.3–4 [Ulpian].

[3] Dig. Just. 1.1.7.1 (Papinian).

[4] Dig. Just. 1.1.6.1 (Ulpian).

[5] Inst. Just. 1.2.3.

[6] Dig. Just. 1.3.1 (Papinian).

[7] Code Just. 1.19.2 (Constantine).

[8] Dig. Just. 1.3.31 [Ulpian]; Code Just. 6.23.3 (Alexander).

[9] Dig. Just. 10.4.19 (Paul); Dig. Just. 1.3.18 (Celsus).

32. On the expansion of laws outside themselves, or on the continued effect of the reason for laws on their further definition. Analogous application.[10] Difference between this and expansive interpretation.[11]

33. On the continued effect of the ground of laws on the law. Can the stopping of the reason avoid stopping the law?

34. Conflict of laws.

35. Application of laws. Influence of natural law, morals, equity to the application of laws.

36. On the way laws stop and their repeal.

37. On custom, jus non scriptum. Origin and exigencies. Relation to Roman and Canon Law and to imperial laws. Evidence of custom.[12] Observance.

38. On judicial custom.[13]

39. On laws in the form of singularity. As entitlement of a single class or as negation of jus commune, jus singulare, as entitlement of singles in general, as the whole single law, privilegium.

40. Kinds of Privileges. Their effects.

41. Transition from privilege to law in subjective relation.

Second Chapter: On Law in Subjective Relation

42. On law as subject, or the person. On the difference between men and person in Roman Law.[14] On the equality of the two.

43. On the physical life of the person. Birth,[15] difference between sexes.[16] Health, bodily as well as mental. Age. Presence. Absence. Domicilium.

44. On the person as regards his or her reputation. Minutio, consumtio existimationis.[17]

45. On infamia [defamation]. Kinds [of defamation]. Infamia juris et facti.[18] Immediata, mediata.

46. On the levis notae macula. Contemporary view. Notoriety and dishonesty.

47. Cancellation of infamia.

---

[10] Dig. Just. 1.3.12 (Julian); Dig. Just. 1.3.13 (Ulpian).

[11] Dig. Just. 50.17.141 (Paul); Dig. Just. 50.17.162 [Paul].

[12] Dig. Just. 1.3.32.pr–1 (Julian); Dig. Just. 1.3.33 (Ulpian); Code Just. 8.53.2 (Constantine).

[13] Dig. Just. 1.3.38 (Callistratus); Code Just. 7.45.13 (Justinian).

[14] Dig. Just. 50.17.209 (Ulpian); Dig. Just. 50.17.32 (Ulpian).

[15] Dig. Just. 1.5.14 (Paul); Dig. Just. 1.5.7 (Paul); Dig. Just. 50.16.231 (Paul).

[16] Dig. Just. 1.5.10 (Ulpian); Dig. Just. 50.16.1 (Paul) [*sic*] [Ulpian]; Dig. Just. 50.16.195 (Ulpian); Dig. Just. 5.1.12.2 (Paul).

[17] Dig. Just. 50.13.5.1–3 (Callistratus).

[18] Dig. Just. 50.16.42 (Ulpian); Dig. Just. 37.15.2–2.1 (Ulpian) [*sic*] [Julian]; Dig. Just. 3.2.20 (Papinian); Code Just. 12.1.2 (Alexander).

48. On death. Presumption in favor of life.[19]

49. On the abstraction of a moral or juridical person.[20] Different kinds.

50. On the tax authority.[21]

51. On other juridical persons.[22]

52. The person as legal subject in relationship to objective law. The person must exist under the law [im Rechte sein], i.e., first and foremost, must know the law.

53. Difference between ignorance of law and of fact. Effect of each.[23]

54. On the restoration of law. Transition to legal procedure.

Third Chapter: Realization of Law, or on Legal Procedure

55. On the most immediate and thus unjust manner of obtaining justice, or on *self-help*. Difference between self-help and self-defense.[24]

56. Penalties for self-help. On Decretum Divi Marci[25] and other ordinances.

57. Resort to judicial mediation. Complaint.[26]

58. On the different classification and kinds of complaints [or actions] in relation to the source of law, procedure, and legal content. Actiones civiles, honorariae.[27] Directae, utiles, in factum.[28] Directae, contrariae.[29] Actiones praejudiciales in rem, in personam, in rem scriptae – stricti juris bonae fidei, arbitrariae – rei presequutoriae, poenales et mixtae.

59. On the cause of action. Concurrence of complaint.[30]

60. On active and passive transmission of the complaint.

61. Expiration of cause of action by means of statute of limitations – praescriptio. Time and the requirement for it. Interruption and inactivity.

62. On the defence to the complaint by the denial [or demurrer], exceptio.[31]

---

19 Dig. Just. 34.5.9(10) (Tryphoninus); Dig. Just. 35.2.68 (Aemilius Macer).

20 Dig. Just. 50.1.25 (Ulpian).

21 Dig. Just. 49.14.6 (Ulpian); Dig. Just. 49.14.37 (Papinian).

22 Dig. Just. 3.4.1.1 (Gaius); Code Just. 10.10.1 (Diocletian and Maximian); Dig. Just. 4.2.9.1 (Ulpian); Dig. Just. 4.3.15.1 (Ulpian); Dig. Just. 43.16.4 (Ulpian).

23 Dig. Just. 22.6.1.pr–3 (Paul); Dig. Just. 22.6.2 (Neratius); Dig. Just. 22.6.3.pr–1 (Pomponius); Dig. Just. 22.6.7 (Papinian); Dig. Just. 22.6.8 [Papinian]; Dig. Just. 22.6.9 (Paul).

24 Dig. Just. 42.8.10.16 (Ulpian).

25 Dig. Just. 48.7.7 (Callistratus).

26 Dig. Just. 44.7.37 (Ulpian).

27 Dig. Just. 44.7.35 (Paul).

28 Dig. Just. 19.5.1.pr (Papinian).

29 Dig. Just. 27.4.1 [Ulpian]; Dig. Just. 13.6.17.1 (Paul); Dig. Just. 13.6.18.4 (Gaius); Dig. Just. 3.5.7(8) (Ulpian).

30 Dig. Just. 44.7.34 (Paul).

31 Dig. Just. 44.1.2 (Ulpian); Dig. Just. 44.1.20 (Paul).

63. Classification and kinds of exceptions.[32]

64. On the relationship of the denial to the complaint and on the effectiveness of the denial.[33]

65. On the negation of the denial. Plaintiff's replication.[34] Restriction of the unending continuation of this negation. Defendant's rejoinder.

66. On the transition from particular procedural actions to procedure as a whole. Litis contestatio, judicium acceptum.

67. On the nature and effect of litis contestatio.

68. On the contemporary meaning of litis contestatio.

69. On evidence. Establishing proof (*Beweissatz*). Means of proof. Argument. Burden of proof.

70. On evidentiary presumption. Praesumptiones.

71. On praesumtio juris et de jure. On praesumtio juris. On praesumtio hominis.[35]

72. On the means of proof. Witnesses and experts. Documents. Oath.

73. On the different kinds and connections of oaths.

74. On confessio.[36]

75. On interrogationes in jure.[37] Its contemporary use.

76. On the completion of legal process, or on the decision.

77. On the authority to decide – jurisdictio – imperium merum and mixtum. Contested and voluntary jurisdiction.

78. On the judgment – res judicata.

79. On the influence of subjective relationships to the rendering of judgment – Condemnatio in id, quod facere potest, beneficium competentiae.

80. On providing security for the judicial decision. Different ways of providing security.

81. On the security granted by the judge. Missio in possessionem. Attachment.

82. On the security provided by the parties. Bond. Sequestratio.

83. Entitlement of the person to a right that has been lost. Reinstatement in the previous situation, restitutio in integrum. Principle of restitution.[38]

84. The restitutio in integrum as directed against the universal right rests on particular grounds. On these particular grounds.[39]

---

[32] Dig. Just. 44.1.7.pr–1 (Paul); Dig. Just. 44.4.2.5 (Ulpian); Dig. Just. 44.1.3 (Gaius).

[33] Dig. Just. 44.4.2.pr–2 (Ulpian).

[34] Dig. Just. 44.1.22.1 (Paul).

[35] Dig. Just. 22.3.26 (Papinian).

[36] Dig. Just. 42.2.1 (Paul); Dig. Just. 42.2.4 (Paul).

[37] Dig. Just. 11.1.1.pr–1 (Callistratus).

[38] Dig. Just. 4.1.1 (Ulpian).

[39] Dig. Just. 4.4.16.pr–1 (Ulpian); Dig. Just. 4.4.16.2 (Pomponius) [*sic*] [Ulpian]; Dig. Just. 4.4.44 (Ulpian).

85. Restitution on account of infancy.[40] Extension to cities and churches.
86. Restitution on account of legal absence from the jurisdiction.
87. Restitution on account of coercion, fraud, mistake, capitis deminutio.[41]
88. Restitution for general grounds – ex clausula generali.[42]
89. On the suit for restitution.
90. On the effects of restitution.[43]
91. Transition from the restitutio in integrum to the content of law or from law in general to the objects of law, first and foremost to the rights of ownership. Subdivision of these rights. Theory of physical things. Possession. Property. Usufruct and servitudes. Liens – imperfect property (*emphyteusis, superficies*).

Second Book: On Property Law

First Chapter: On Physical Things

92. On physical things as purely external, natural. As such they are not an object of legal science.
93. Physical things as object (*Gegenstand*) of law presuppose the relation of property.
94. On the physical thing as legal object (*Rechtsobject*) in general.[44]
95. Subdivision and kinds of physical things. Res in commercio and extra commercium and even res divini juris,[45] res communes, res publicae – res corporales, incorporales – res immobiles, mobiles sese moventes – res dividuae, individuae.
96. On physical things in the form of universality – res fungibiles. Money.[46]
97. On physical things in the form of ideal totality – universitates rerum.[47]
98. On the physical thing in relation to another physical thing. Accessories. Secondary things [or claims (*Nebensache*)].

---

[40] Dig. Just. 4.4.13.1 (Ulpian); Dig. Just. 4.4.12 (Gaius); Dig. Just. 4.4.24.1 (Ulpian); Code Just. 2.25.2 (Alexander).
[41] Dig. Just. 4.5.2.1 (Ulpian).
[42] Dig. Just. 4.6.1.1 (Ulpian); Dig. Just. 4.6.26.9 (Ulpian).
[43] Dig. Just. 4.4.41 (Julian).
[44] Dig. Just. 50.16.23 (Ulpian).
[45] Dig. Just. 11.7.2.4 (Ulpian); Dig. Just. 11.7.44 (Paul).
[46] Dig. Just. 18.1.1.pr (Paul).
[47] Dig. Just. 41.3.30.2 (Pomponius).

99. On the accessory as *organic* development of the physical thing. *Crops* – fructus naturales – civiles.[48] Different condition and multiple relations of crops.

100. On the accessory as absorbed by the physical thing. *Improvements* – impensae, expensae. Different relations according to the measure of necessity,[49] utility, ornamentation.

101. On the accessory in the form of mechanical, external and divisible connection. *Appurtenances*.

102. On the physical thing in relationship to the person. Transition to possession.

Second Chapter: On Possession

103. Presentation of different prevailing opinions on possession. Possession is no mere factum, and it does not arise as *law* by the circuitous path of *injustice*.

104. Possession as property from the side of the merely particular will. *Incipient*, presumptive property.[50]

105. On the effects derived from the concept of possession. On the protection of possession, *Interdicts*. On the possibility of possession becoming property. *Ususcapion*. Are there other effects of possession?

106. Subdivision and kinds of possession – possessio justa and injusta. Validity of this subdivision for possession[51] – bonae and malae fidei possessio – possessio civilis, possessio naturalis, possessio, civiliter non possidere.[52] On the rule nemo causam possessionis sibi mutare potest.[53]

107. On the objects of possession. Juris quasi possessio.

108. Subjective requirements of possession. Animus domini. Exceptions.[54] Acquisition by agent – constitutum possessorium.[55] Physically holding[56] – traditio brevi manu. Possession in single parts of a physical thing – possessio plurium in solidum.[57]

---

48 Dig. Just. 50.16.121 (Pomponius).

49 Dig. Just. 25.1.1.pr–3 (Ulpian).

50 Dig. Just. 4.6.19 (Papinian); Dig. Just. 41.2.1.1–3 (Paul); Dig. Just. 41.2.1.4 [Paul]; Dig. Just. 50.16.78 [Paul].

51 Dig. Just. 41.2.3.5 (Ulpian).

52 Dig. Just. 10.4.3.15 (Ulpian); Dig. Just. 43.16.1.9–10 (Ulpian); Dig. Just. 41.3.16 (Javolenus); Dig. Just. 24.2.26 (Paul); Dig. Just. 41.6.1.2 (Paul).

53 Dig. Just. 41.9.2.1 (Julian).

54 Dig. Just. 13.7.37 (Paul); Dig. Just. 16.3.17.1 (Florentinus).

55 Dig. Just. 41.2.18 (Celsus).

56 Dig. Just. 18.1.74 (Papinian).

57 Dig. Just. 41.2.3.5 (Paul).

109. Loss of possession. By animus. By a factum contrarium.[58] Loss of possession to an agent.

110. On the means of protecting possession, on the interdicts. Interdicta retinendae possessionis. Interdicta recuperandae possessionis, *cause of action for spoils* [*Spolienklage*].

111. Transition from possession as incipient property to perfect property.

Third Chapter: On Property

112. Concept of property as the external sphere of freedom. Difference from possession. The person must have property.

113. Object of property. Material physical things – intellectual property.

114. Exclusiveness of property. There is only a perfect property. On the differences and kinds of property that occur in it.

115. Kinds of property. Dominium, bonae fidei possessio. Dominium directum and utile.[59]

116. Methods of acquiring property and specifically

A) immediate acquisition;

B) acquisition mediated by change in the physical thing;

C) acquisition mediated by the will of another.

117. A) Immediate acquisition and specifically 1) that which takes the person to the physical thing – occupation (treasure trove, booty, hunting, fishing) – or that 2) which takes the physical thing to the property – accession – its different kinds and relations.[60]

118. B) Acquisition mediated by change in the physical thing – fabrication (*Formation*) and specifically 1) by keeping control over the item fabricated 2) complete change into something new. Change of species (*Specification*).[61]

119. C) Acquisition mediated by the will of another. Tradition and its requirements. Adjudicatio. Adverse possession.

120. Historical introduction to adverse possession. Its concept.

121. On the objects of adverse possession.[62]

122. On possession[63] – accessio possessionis. On the calculation of time – tempus continuum, utile – civil rules for the computation of time.[64]

---

[58] Dig. Just. 50.17.153 (Paul).

[59] Dig. Just. 6.3.1.1 (Paul).

[60] Dig. Just. 41.1.31.1 (Paul); Dig. Just. 41.1.7.2–3 (Gaius); Dig. Just. 6.1.23.4–5 (Paul).

[61] Inst. Just. 2.1.25–26.

[62] Dig. Just. 8.6.10.pr (Paul); Code Just. 7.26.9 (Philip); Dig. Just. 44.4.4.24–24a (Ulpian); Dig. Just. 27.5.2 (Celsus); Dig. Just. 41.1.48 (Paul); Dig. Just. 41.4.2.15 (Paul).

[63] Dig. Just. 41.4.6.2 (Pomponius).

[64] Dig. Just. 44.3.15 (Venuleius).

123. On bona fides.[65]

124. On the objective ground of possession – justus titulus.[66] Particular titles.

125. On the interruption [or tolling] of the statute of limitations.[67]

126. On extraordinary adverse possession.[68]

127. On some other supposed kinds of acquiring.

128. Absolute relation of the owner to the property. Restriction [or qualification] of this. Prohibitions on alienation.

129. Means of protecting property – rei vindicatio. Requirements and conditions of it, both as regards the plaintiff and defendant, and as regards the principal cause of action and the secondary claim.[69]

130. On the obligatory relationships which serve partly as preparation, partly as replacement for the rei vindicatio – actio ad exhibendum[70] – actio de tigno juncto.

131. On the actio Publiciana.[71]

132. On the exceptio rei traditae ac venditae.[72]

133. On the actio negatoria.[73]

134. The property owner relinquishes particular aspects of the property. Relinquishment of enjoyment. Relinquishment of exclusive use. The aspect relinquished becomes an independent right – usufruct, servitudes.

Fourth Chapter: On Usufruct and Servitudes

135. On the conceptual diversity between usufruct and servitudes, which accordingly are not included as parts of one and the same whole. On the classification into personal and real servitudes.

A. On Usufruct

136. Usufruct as the use or enjoyment *separated* from the ownership.[74]

---

65 Dig. Just. 41.3.25 (Pomponius); Dig. Just. 50.16.109 (Modestinus); Dig. Just. 41.1.48.1 (Paul); Dig. Just.41.2.43.pr–2 (Marcian).

66 Dig. Just. 41.3.27 (Ulpian).

67 Dig. Just. 41.3.5 (Gaius).

68 Code Just. 7.39.8.pr–1 (Justinian).

69 Dig. Just. 6.1.23.pr–2 (Paul); Dig. Just. 6.1.6 (Paul); Dig. Just. 24.1.55 (Paul); Dig. Just. 6.1.80 (Furius Anthianus); Dig. Just. 6.1.62.1 (Papinian); Dig. Just. 41.3.4.19–20 (Paul).

70 Dig. Just. 6.1.23.5 (Paul); Dig. Just. 10.4.3.11 [Ulpian]; Dig. Just. 10.4.6 (Paul).

71 Dig. Just. 6.6.1.1 (Ulpian); Dig. Just. 6.2.1.1 (Ulpian).

72 Dig. Just. 21.3.1.2 (Ulpian); Dig. Just. 21.3.2 (Pomponius).

73 Dig. Just. 7.6.5.pr (Ulpian).

74 Dig. Just. 44.2.21.3 (Pomponius).

137. Of the relation of both parts, fructus and usus, in usufruct.[75]

138. On quasi-usufruct.[76]

139. On the rights and obligations of the usufructuary in relation to use and disposition.[77]

140. On the right of usus.[78]

141. On the right of habitatio. Operae.

142. Common relations of usufruct, usus, habitatio, and operae. Differences. On the arrangement of these rights. On security interests.[79]

143. On the termination of these rights in relation to the principle of their subjectivity.

B. *On Servitudes*

144. On the principle of servitudes. Their relationship to property.[80]

145. Classification and kinds of servitudes – servitutes praediorum urbanorum – servitutes praediorum rusticorum. Particular servitudes.[81]

146. Ways of creating servitudes. Can they be created by mere contract?[82]

147. On possession of servitudes.

148. On acquisition of servitudes by adverse possession.[83]

149. Ways of protecting servitudes – actio confessoria – negatoria.

150. On the termination of servitudes. Destruction of the object – confusio and consolidatio. Abandonment. Nonuse.[84]

151. The owner can relinquish the occupation [or possession (*Innehabung*)] and certainty of his or her property just as he can relinquish its exclusive use. Transition to the liens.

---

75 Dig. Just. 7.8.14.1 (Ulpian); Dig. Just. 7.8.14.3 (Ulpian); Dig. Just. 7.9.5.1–2 (Ulpian); Dig. Just. 46.4.13.3 (Ulpian).

76 Dig. Just. 7.5.1 (Ulpian); Dig. Just. 7.9.9.3 (Ulpian).

77 Dig. Just. 7.1.59.1 (Paul); Dig. Just. 7.1.13.5 (Ulpian); Dig. Just. 7.1.9.4 (Ulpian); Dig. Just. 7.1.61 (Neratius).

78 Dig. Just. 7.8.22.pr–1 (Pomponius); Dig. Just. 7.8.12.4 [Ulpian].

79 Dig. Just. 7.1.56 (Gaius).

80 Dig. Just. 8.1.15.1 (Pomponius); Dig. Just. 8.5.6.2

81 (Ulpian).Dig. Just. 8.2.38 (Paul); Dig. Just. 8.2.39 [Paul]; Dig. Just. 8.2.2 (Gaius).

82 Inst. Just. 2.3.4; Inst. Just. 2.4.1; Dig. Just. 7.4.1 (Ulpian); Dig. Just. 7.1.3 (Gaius); Dig. Just. 6.2.11.1 (Ulpian).

83 Dig. Just. 8.1.14 (Paul); Dig. Just. 8.5.10 (Ulpian).

84 Dig. Just. 8.3.34.pr (Papinian); Dig. Just. 8.2.6 [Gaius].

Fifth Chapter: On Liens

152. On the lien as possession, certainty, and security that have been severed from the property. Meaning of the word pignus. Difference between pignus and hypotheca.[85]

153. On the prerequisites for the lien. Debt.[86]

154. On the objects of the lien. Pignus generale, speciale.[87]

A. Acquisition of the Lien

155. On the ways of creating the lien. Pignus voluntarium (conventionale testamentarium), pignus necessarium (legale tacitum, and praetorium judiciale).

156. On the lien created by covenant.[88]

157. On the lien created by testament.

158. On pignus necessarium, and specifically the pignus tacitum. On privilegium exigendi.

159. On special liens created by statute.[89]

160. On general statutory liens.

B. Legal Relationship of the Lienholder to the Owner and to Joint Creditors

161. Relationship of the lienholder to the owner. Priority of title as against a third party. Right of alienation.

162. On the alienation of the lien. Creation of secondary liens.[90]

163. On the sale of the collateral. Necessary conditions. Effects of the sale. On the purchase of the collateral by the creditor. Lex Commissoria.[91]

164. On the right of retention.

165. On the relationship of the lien holders. *Priority.*

166. On privileged liens created by statute. On privileged liens created by agreement.[92]

---

[85] Dig. Just. 20.1.5.1 (Marcian).

[86] Dig. Just. 20.1.5.pr (Marcian).

[87] Dig. Just. 20.1.6 (Ulpian).

[88] Dig. Just. 13.7.1 (Ulpian); Dig. Just. 13.7.41 (Paul); Dig. Just. 20.1.22 (Modestinus); Dig. Just. 20.3.4 (Paul); Dig. Just. 20.4.12.2 (Marcian).

[89] Dig. Just. 20.2.1 (Papinian); Dig. Just. 27.9.3.pr (Ulpian); Code Just. 7.8.6 (Alexander); Dig. Just. 20.4.7.pr (Ulpian).

[90] Dig. Just. 20.1.13.2 (Marcian); Code Just. 8.24.2 (Diocletian and Maximian).

[91] Dig. Just. 13.7.4 (Ulpian); Dig. Just. 20.5.7.pr–1 Marcian).; Code Just. 8.34.3.1–3 (Justinian); Dig. Just. 42.1.15.3 (Ulpian).

[92] Dig. Just. 49.14.28 (Ulpian); Dig. Just. 20.4.21 (Scaevola); Code Just. 7.73.2 (Alexander) [*sic*] [Antoninus].

167. On the relationship of public liens and private liens.[93]

168. On the priority of time.[94] On the priority of possession.

169. On the rights of lien holders who come later – jus offerendi.[95]

170. On ways of protecting the lien – actio hypothecaria, its statute of limitations – interdictum Salvianum.

C. Extinction of the Lien

171. I. Immediate extinction. Destruction of the object. Confusion.[96]

172. II. Mediated methods of extinction – remissio pignoris – usucapio libertatis.

173. III. Extinction by the nature of the relationship of the collateral. Redemption of the principal obligation. Sale of the collateral.[97]

174. The property remains property, while burdened with usufruct, servitudes and lien – naked property. Over against that, the property of mere enjoyment and of restricted right of transfer appears as imperfect property.

175. Transition to Emphyteusis and Superficies.

Sixth Chapter: On Emphyteusis and Superficies

176. On the historical origin and the significance of emphyteusis – ager vectigalis.

177. On the establishment of emphyteusis.[98]

178. Rights of the emphyteuta in relationship to use and disposition.

179. On the independence of the emphyteuta.

180. On legal remedies available for the emphyteuticary relationship.

181. Termination of the relationship. Destruction of the object – confusio – dereliction. Statute of Limitation. Privation.

182. On the significance of superficies. Relationship to property and to emphyteusis.[99]

183. On the origin of superficies.

184. On the rights of the superficiarus.

185. On the legal remedies incident thereto.

186. On the expiration of the superficies.

---

[93] Code Just. 8.18.11 (Leo).

[94] Dig. Just. 20.4.11.pr–1 (Gaius).

[95] Dig. Just. 20.4.20 (Tryphoninus).

[96] Dig. Just. 20.1.16.2 (Marcian); Dig. Just. 20.6.3 (Ulpian).

[97] Dig. Just. 20.6.6.pr (Ulpian); Dig. Just. 13.7.24.3

[98] (Ulpian).Code Just. 4.66.1 (Zeno).

[99] Dig. Just. 43.18.1.pr–2 (Ulpian).

---

187. The person does not just extricate himself from particular incidents of property, but rather the person declares himself for the first time truly as owner through *alienation*.

188. On alienation in the form of mere abandonment [*Aufgebens*]. Derelictio. On alienation in the form of transfer. Acquisition of another [...] by means of the owner.

189. Property ceases to be immediate and absolute. Mediation of property. Transition to the law of obligations.

THIRD BOOK: ON THE LAW OF OBLIGATIONS

First Chapter: On Obligations in General

190. Concept of the law of obligations. Property turns into a body of economic law. The person owes something to the person.[100]

191. On the connection of the obligatio and actio under Roman Law. Obligationes stricti juris, condictiones, obligationes bonae fidei. On the obligationes stricti juris, as regards its origin and effect. On the classification of obligationes bonae fidei. The bonae fidei obligationes are actual obligationes. On the interesse. Concurrence of obligationes stricti juris and bonae fidei. On obligations which are not stricti juris and bonae fidei.[101]

192. Classification and kinds of obligation – obligation civilis and naturalis.[102]

193. On the subjects of obligatio. Correal-obligations. [?][103]

194. On the objects of obligatio – obligation alternativa.[104]

195. The characteristic of obligatio that there is not merely one obligatio as property but rather an organization and gradation of obligations. The relationship of person to person arises partly by mediation, partly by violation of the will. Contract, Delict.

196. Classification of obligations into contracts and delicts. Transition to contracts.

---

[100] Dig. Just. 44.7.3.pr (Paul).

[101] Dig. Just. 50.16.19 (Ulpian); Dig. Just. 13.3.1.pr–1 (Ulpian); Dig. Just. 45.1.75.pr–2 (Ulpian); Dig. Just. 45.1.75.8 (Ulpian); Inst. Just. 4.6.28; Dig. Just. 19.1.11.6 (Ulpian); Dig. Just. 12.1.9.pr–1 (Ulpian).

[102] Dig. Just. 50.17.84.1 (Paul); Dig. Just. 45.1.1.2 (Ulpian); Dig. Just. 46.3.95.4 (Papinian).

[103] Dig. Just. 45.2.9.pr (Papinian).

[104] Dig. Just. 45.1.76 (Paul); Dig. Just. 45.1.141 (Gaius).

Second Chapter: On Contracts and Similar Obligatory Relationships

197. On contract. Difference between contract and promise. Pollicitatio, votum.

198. Difference between contractus and pacta under Roman Law.[105]

199. On consensus as the foundation of contract. On the form of contract.

200. On the construction of contracts.[106]

201. On the influence of error on the contract.[107]

202. On the influence of coercion and fraud on the contract. On the influence of counterfeiting.

203. On the independence of the contract. Conditions. Conditions precedent. Conditions that excuse performance. [*Resolutivbedingung* means a resolutory condition or a dissolving condition or condition that causes a contract to lapse.] Physically and morally impossible conditions. Effects of conditions. Time of performance. Dies [day of performance].

204. On the confirmation of the contract. Arrha. Liquidated damages.[108] Oath.

205. The contract is not merely one [thing] like property; there is rather an organization and gradation in contracts.

206. On the Roman Law classification of contracts as real, verbal, literal, and consensual contracts. On the hitherto customary classification.

207. On the classification that proceeds from the nature of the contract. Formal contract, contract of donation. Real contract, barter agreement. Contracts completely executed by both parties.

A. *Formal Contracts or Contracts of Donation*

1) Gift of a Physical Thing – Donatio.

208. Concept of donatio. Its acceptance.[109]

209. On donatio remuneratoria. On donatio sub modo. On donatio omnium bonorum. On the binding obligation to deliver (*Eviction zu leisten*).[110]

210. On the retraction [revocation] of the gift.

---

[105] Dig. Just. 2.14.7.1.pr–2 (Ulpian).

[106] Dig. Just. 2.14.39 (Papinian); Dig. Just. 45.1.38.18 (Ulpian); Dig. Just. 18.1.34 (Paul); Dig. Just. 19.1.54.1 (Labeo).

[107] Dig. Just. 44.7.57 (Pomponius); Dig. Just. 18.1.9 (Ulpian).

[108] Dig. Just. 19.1.28 (Julian).

[109] Dig. Just. 39.5.9 (Pomponius).

[110] Dig. Just. 39.5.18.3 (Ulpian); Code Just. 8.45.2 (Severus and Antoninus); Dig. Just. 32.29.3 (Labeo); Dig. Just. 30.45.1.pr–2 (Pomponius); Dig. Just. 30.46 [Pomponius]; Dig. Just. 21.2.58 (Javolenus); Opinions of Paul 5.11.5; Dig. Just. 6.1.48 (Papinian); Dig. Just. 45.1.131.1 (Scaevola).

2) Gift of Use (Commodatum Precarium, Mutuum)

211. On the gratuitous loan of a specific physical thing. Commodatum. Respective [reciprocal or mutual] rights and duties of the persons participating therein.[111]

212. On the solicited loan [or loan for the benefit of the borrower] of a particular physical thing. Precarium. Its nature.

213. On the gratuitous loan of a universal [fungible or interchangeable?] physical thing. Mutuum. Its acceptance.[112]

214. On the Senatusconsultum Macedonianum.

215. On the obligatory relationships that are similar to mutuum as regards their effect – repetitio, condictio ob causam.

216. Different kinds. Condictio indebiti, condictio causa data, causa non secuta, condictio ob turpem causam, condictio furtiva, condictio sine causa.

217. On the exceptio non numeratae pecuniae in connection with the loan.

3) Gift of Services

218. On the gift of services of safekeeping. Depositum. Nature and acceptance of the contract. On deponens and depositarius. Rights and duties of the two. On depositum irregulare. On depositum miserabile.[113]

219. On the gift of services in general in the form of a request [or mandate or commission or gratuitous contract (*Auftrag*)]. Mandatum. Difference from depositum and conflict with it.[114]

220. On the nature of the mandate.[115] Consilium. Mandatum qualificatum. Allotment.

221. On the rights and duties of the mandans and mandatarius.

222. On the grounds for cancelling the mandate. Death. Revocation.[116]

223. On the negotiorum gestio. Difference from mandate. Relationships of the participants therein.[117]

224. On the actio funeraria.

---

111 Dig. Just. 13.6.1 (Ulpian).

112 Dig. Just. 12.1.2.pr–1 (Paul); Dig. Just. 12.1.32 (Celsus); Dig. Just. 12.1.11.1.pr–2 (Ulpian).

113 Dig. Just. 12.1.9.9 (Ulpian); Dig. Just. 12.1.10 (Ulpian).

114 Dig. Just. 16.3.1.1.11–13 (Ulpian).

115 Dig. Just. 17.1.4 (Paul); Dig. Just. 17.2.6 (Gaius).

116 Dig. Just. 46.3.108 (Paul).

117 Dig. Just. 3.5.9(10).1 (Ulpian).

B. Agreements of Exchange

1) Exchange as Such

225. a) Exchange of a specific physical thing for another – permutatio.

226. b) Exchange of reciprocal requests. Accord or compromise – transactio. Difference from mere renunciation. Requirements and effects of the accord.[118]

227. On compromissum. Relation of compromissum to accord. On receptum. On the effect in connection to the parties.[119]

228. c) Exchange of speculative expectancies. Gambling. Betting.[120]

229. d) Exchange of a specific physical thing for its value. Sale – emtio venditio.

230. On the persons of the buyer and the seller. Acceptance of the sale. Objects of the sale.[121]

231. On price, pretium. Relationship of the price to the value – laesio enormis – cancellation on this ground.

232. On the effects of this contract. Transfer of ownership. Accomplishing eviction. Edict of the aediles.[122]

233. On the specific kinds of purchase. Sale to the highest offer. Purchase at the lowest price. Purchase of a debt due. Purchase of income generated by an estate.[123]

234. On the pactis adjectis, which results also from other contracts but mostly from purchases – pactum displicentiae – pactum de retrovendendo – pactum de retroemendo – jus protimiseos – in diem addictio. Lex commissoria.[124]

2) Exchange of the Use of a Physical Thing for Its Value

235. a) Alienation of the use of a property from rent – locatio conductio.

236. Requirements and nature of the lease agreement. Rights and duties of the lessor and lessee. On the remittal. Conditions of lease. On leasing property out again.[125]

---

118 Dig. Just. 2.15.14 (Scaevola).

119 Dig. Just. 4.8.17.5–7 (Ulpian).

120 Dig. Just. 11.5.1.pr (Ulpian); Dig. Just. 11.5.2.1 (Paul).

121 Dig. Just. 18.1.34.1 (Paul).

122 Dig. Just. 19.1.30.1 (Africanus); Dig. Just. 21.1.1.2–3 (Ulpian).

123 Dig. Just. 18.1.81.1 (Scaevola).

124 Dig. Just. 18.2.7 (Paul); Dig. Just. 18.2.8 [Paul]; Dig. Just. 42.5.16 (Gaius).

125 Dig. Just. 19.2.2 (Gaius); Dig. Just. 19.2.25.6 (Gaius); Dig. Just. 19.2.32 (Julian); Dig. Just. 19.2.27.1 (Alfenus); Dig. Just. 19.2.13.11 (Ulpian).

237. b) Lease of a universal physical thing. Loan with interest.

238. On interest – usurae. Kinds of interest. Permitted interest – usurae usurarum.

239. On interusurium. Different ways of calculation.

240. On foenus nauticum.

3) Exchange of a Service for Its Value (Locatio Operarum)

241. On locatio operarum – locatio conductio operis. Some principles.

242. On actio exercitoria.

243. On actio institoria.

244. On the Lex Rhodia de jactu.[126]

245. On contractus aestimatorius.[127]

246. On suffragium.

247. On the so-called innominatcontracts and the jus poenitendi.[128]

C. Completed Contracts

1) Completion of the Subject of the Contracts within Itself (Societas)

248. Concept of [legal] association. Its creation. Rights and duties of socii with respect to each other. Relationship of the socii with respect to a third party. Kinds of association. Termination of the association.[129]

249. On the communio incidens. Ways of creating it. Difference from the association. General principles. Its purpose [*Prinzip*] is to cease to exist. Partition.

250. On the action for partition – actio communi dividundo[130] – actio familiae erciscundae – actio finium regundorum.

2) Completion of the Object of the Contract within Itself

251. a) By ratification – constitutum debiti proprii. Its requirements and effects.

252. b) By hypothecation and specifically by personal hypothecation – pledge for the debt of another, suretyship – as well as by objective hypothecation – *actual pledge*.

126 Dig. Just. 14.2.1–2 (Paul).

127 Dig. Just. 19.3.pr–1 (Ulpian).

128 Dig. Just. 19.5.pr–5 (Paul); Dig. Just. 12.4.3.2–3 (Ulpian); Dig. Just. 12.4.5 (Ulpian).

129 Dig. Just. 17.2.31 (Pomponius) [*sic*] [Ulpian]; Dig. Just. 17.2.32 (Pomponius) [*sic*] [Ulpian]; Dig. Just. 17.2.29.2 (Ulpian).

130 Dig. Just. 10.3.4 (Ulpian); Dig. Just. 17.2.34 (Gaius); Dig. Just. 10.1.11 (Papinian).

253. On pledge for the debt of another in general – its concept and kinds.

254. On suretyship (fidejussio). Relationship to the principal obligation and to the party primarily obligated. Beneficia grounded thereon.[131]

255. On mandatum qualificatum.

256. On constitutum debiti alieni.

257. Restrictions on pledges for the debt of another on other grounds. Pledges for the debt of another or womankind. On the Senatusconsultum Velleianum.[132] On the form of an instrumenti publici.

258. On the contract of pledge. On the rights and duties of the lienholder and the pledgor. On the pactum antichreticum.

---

259. Contracts *contain* specifically the mediation of the will, but nevertheless the side of the particular will of the person is preserved in it. From the side of the particular will the contract remains a property of the contracting parties, and the question arises: who bears the casus?

260. On periculum and commodum. Relationship and principles.

261. From the side of the particular will the contract is also violated, and specifically by the determinate wrong of delayed performance – mora, or by every wrong in general – dolus, culpa.

262. On mora – mora solvendi – mora accipiendi. Effects of mora. Purgatio morae.[133]

263. On dolus and on culpa. Relationship of both.

264. On culpa as the source of obligatio. On culpa as appearing within an extant obligatio. On the classification of culpa into culpa in faciendo and culpa non faciendo.

265. On the degrees of culpa. On the three degrees – culpa lata – culpa levis. On diligentia in concreto and diligentia in abstracto.[134]

266. On the discharge of culpa. On the proof of culpa.

267. Dolus and culpa are the destruction of the obligation in the contractual relationship, but then they are in turn the foundation of obligations which accordingly have dolus and culpa as their contents. Obligations ex delicto.

---

131 Dig. Just. 46.1.8.7–8 (Ulpian).

132 Dig. Just. 16.1.2.1 (Ulpian); Code Just. 4.29.3 (Justinian).

133 Dig. Just. 22.1.32 (Marcian).

134 Dig. Just. 16.3.32 (Celsus); Dig. Just. 50.16.213.2 (Ulpian); Dig. Just. 13.6.5.2–3 (Ulpian); Dig. Just. 50.17.23 (Ulpian).

Third Chapter: On Delicts and Related Obligatory Relationships

268. On obligations which have as their basis an injury of the will – obligationes ex delicto – obligationes quasi ex delicto. On civil penalty and its purpose [*Prinzip*].

269. These obligations rest partly on merely possible injury – prophylactic or police obligations – partly on actual injury – true obligationes ex delicto.

A. Prophylactic Obligatory Relationships Which Rest on the Possibility of an Injury

270. On cautio damni infecti – missio ex primo, ex secundo Decreto. Effects.[135]

171. [*sic*]. On operis novi nunciatio. Repeal. On nunciatio realis and publica.

272. On actio aquae pluviae arcendae.

273. Interdicta prohibitoria, and specifically a) to the protection of a legal and permitted undertaking – interdictum de loco publico fruendo – interdictum de mortuo inferendo – interdictum de sepulchro aedificando – de locis et itineribus publicis – interdictum de via publica et itinere publico reficiendo – interdictum ut in flumine publico navigare liceat. Interdictum de migrando. Interdictum de itinere actuque privato – interdictum de aqua quotidiana et aestiva – aqua ex castello. Interdictum de fonte. Interdictum de cloacis. Interdictum de arboribus caedendi. Interdictum de glande legenda. b) As prohibition of a wrongful act – interdictum ne quid in loco sacro fiat – interdictum ne quid in loco publico fiat – interdictum ne quid in flumine publico fiat, quo aliter aqua fluat, atque uti priore aestate fluxit – viae receptae actio.

274. On the actio de positis et suspensis.

275. On the binding force of nautae, caupones, and stabularii[136] – actio de receptis – actio furti adversus nautas.

B. Obligations Which Rest on an Actual Injury

276. I. Immediate injury of the person – injuria in the broader meaning – in the narrower meaning – actio legis Corneliae. The praetorian lawsuit for approximate damages.[137]

---

[135] Dig. Just. 39.2.7 (Ulpian).

[136] Dig. Just. 4.9.1.pr–1 (Ulpian); Dig. Just. 4.9.3.1 (Ulpian).

[137] *Si quis tabulas testamenti apud se depositas, pluribus praesentibus, legit. ait Labeo depositi actione recte de tabulis agi posse ego arbitror, et injuriarum agi posse, si hoc animo recitatum testamentum est quibusdam praesentibus, ut judicia secreta ejus, qui testatus est, divulgarentur.* Inst. Just. 4.4.7.

277. II. Injury to the person in its property – damnum injuria datum, actio legis Aquiliae. Its extent. Its nature and effect.[138]

278. Damage by animals – actio de pauperie, noxae datio – actio de pastu.[139]

279. On the damage by the judge – si judex litem suam fecerit.

280. On the actio de effusis et ejectis.

281. On theft.[140] Kinds of theft – condictio furtiva – actio rerum amotarum – actio furti – actio arborum furtim caesarum, actio ad versus publicanos.

282. III. Injury of the person with its property – vi bonorum raptorum – damni in turba datum – actio sepulchri violati. Interdictum quod vi aut clam. Transgression against judicial power.

283. On intent – actio de dolo – actio in factum against the Mensor – alienatio judicii mutandi causa – actio in factum de calumnia.

284. Actio quod metus causa. Its operation (or effects).

---

285. All relationships of obligations express themselves so that the subject of the obligatio, or the object, or both change.

Fourth Chapter: On the Movement and Satisfaction of Obligations

A. Alteration of the Subject of the Obligatio

286. The subject of the obligatio is altered when another creditor occupies the position of an earlier creditor. Assignment.

287. Historical observations on assignment (*Cession*). On the subjects of assignment. Assignor – assignee – debtor [debitor cessus]. On the objects of assignment. Restrictions. Effects on the assignor, assignee, and debtor.

288. The subject of the obligatio is altered when another debtor occupies the place of the earlier debtor, and, specifically, when without contract (*Auftrag*) of the principal debtor. Expromissio in this contract. Delegatio.

289. On the requirements and effects of the Expromissio.[141]

290. On the requirements and effects of Delegatio.[142]

[138] Dig. Just. 9.2.5.1 (Ulpian).
[139] Inst. Just. 4.9.pr.
[140] Dig. Just. 47.2.3.pr–2 (Ulpian); Dig. Just. 13.1.7.1 (Ulpian); Dig. Just. 13.1.7.2 (Ulpian).
[141] Dig. Just. 46.2.8.5 (Ulpian).
[142] Dig. Just. 46.2.11.pr–1 (Ulpian).

B. Alteration of the Object of the Obligatio

291. On novation. Its concept and requirements. Effects.[143]

C. Extinction (or Discharge) of the Obligatio

292. I. Cessation of the obligatio. Impossibility of satisfaction by destruction of the object – by cancellation of the interest – by competition and merger [or confusion of rights] – by conditions that cause the contract to dissolve, and final date – by statute of limitations.

293. Cessation of the obligation by cancellation of the subject. Death. Penalty.

294. II. Sublation of the obligation by the existence of another obligatio. Settlement – its subjective and objective requirements. Effects.[144] Sublation by res judicata.

295. Sublation by contracts to discount or change the conditions of payment – mutuus dissensus – contracts to extend or postpone payment.

296. Sublation by unilateral activity. Gratuitous payment and deposit for safekeeping. Notice of termination (or repudiation) – cessio bonorum.[145] Moratorium. Reduction in price obtained by compulsion.

297. III. Satisfaction of an obligatio. Payment, solutio. Effects and proof. Datio in solutum.[146]

298. The person finds its final goal not in financial position and its connections, but rather the person raises itself to an ethical mediation in which financial position is present only as ancillary moment. Transition to Family Law.

299. On the different situation that our Family Law bears to that of Roman Law, so that the Roman Law is here valid only in specific [cases] and not as purpose [*Prinzip*].

---

143 Dig. Just. 46.2.1.pr (Ulpian); Code Just. 8.42.8 (Justinian).

144 Dig. Just. 16.2.15 (Javolenus).

145 Dig. Just. 42.3.6 (Ulpian).

146 Dig. Just. 46.3.1 (Ulpian).

FOURTH BOOK: ON FAMILY LAW

First Chapter: On Marriage

300. On the concept of Roman marriage. Monogamy. Concubinage. The degree to which Roman marriage corresponds to the demands of true order based on custom [*Sittlichkeit*].[147]

A. Celebration of Marriage

301. Physical capacity.
302. Degree of kinship. Impediments to marriage which arise from the proximity of kinship. Relationship by blood; relationship by adoption. Affinity. Relation of Roman, Mosaic, and Canon Law.
303. On the impediments to marriage which lie outside the marriage. Office and estate. Guardianship. Difference in religion. Crime.
304. On the effect of impediments to marriage.
305. On the forms of celebrating marriage.[148] On consent. On betrothal. On the forms of celebrating marriage according to Catholic and Protestant church law.
306. On *putative marriage.*

B. Legal Relations of Marriage

307. Rights and duties of the spouses besides economic relations. Upbringing of children.
308. Principle of economic relations. Their extraordinary character according to Roman Law: they fall into 1) economic relations which are determined by marriage, 2) economic relations to which marriage is indifferent, 3) economic relations to which marriage is an impediment.
309. 1) Economic relations which are determined by marriage. On the dos, res uxoria. Concept and kinds of these – dos profectitia – dos adventitia – dos receptitia.[149]
310. On the duty to provide a dowry [dotiren].[150] Who has this duty. On the redotatio.
311. On the objects of the dos.

---

[147] Dig. Just. 23.2.1 (Modestinus); Inst. Just. 1.9.1; Dig. Just. 34.9.16.1 (Papinian); Dig. Just. 50.16.144 (Paul).
[148] Dig. Just. 23.2.5 (Pomponius).
[149] Dig. Just. 23.3.3 (Ulpian); Dig. Just. 23.3.5.pr–5 (Ulpian).
[150] Dig. Just. 23.2.19 (Marcellus) [*sic*] [Marcian].

312. On the rights of the husband to the dos.[151] On the property – aestimatio venditionis causa, taxationis causa. On the fundus dotalis, prohibition on alienation. Exceptions.

313. On the rights of the wife to the dos.[152]

314. On the dos after dissolution of marriage. Demand for return on legal grounds, and on contractual grounds. Terms of the demand for return. Legal remedy, actio rei uxoriae, actio ex stipulatu. Extent of the obligation to provide restitution.[153]

315. On the donatio propter nuptias. Rights of the husband and wife.

316. II. On economic relations to which marriage is indifferent. Paraphernalia – relations of the husband to it – pacta dotalia.

317. Other economic relations of the spouses, actio legis Aquiliae[154] – actio rerum amotarum.

318. III. On the economic relations to which marriage is an impediment. Gifts between spouses. Prohibition of them, basis of the prohibition. Exceptions. In what cases the gift is valid.[155]

C. *Dissolution of Marriage*

319. Dissolution by death. Civil death. Canon law.

320. Cancellation of marriage. Divorce. Grounds for divorce according to Roman Law. Catholic, Protestant law.

321. On the disadvantages of divorce.

322. Notice and investigation of pregnancy – actio de partu agnoscendo.

323. On the disadvantages of the second marriage for both spouses, and for the woman in particular. Violation of the year of mourning.[156]

324. Marriage, as the beginning of the family, is the assumption of its further development into *paternal power* and *kinship*.

Second Chapter: On Paternal Power and Kinship

325. On the principle of Roman paternal power. Relation to our notions. Parental relation.[157]

---

[151] Dig. Just. 23.3.7.pr–1 (Ulpian); Code Just. 5.12.5 (Alexander); Code Just. 5.12.12 (Diocletian and Maximian).

[152] Dig. Just. 23.4.21 (Julian).

[153] Dig. Just. 24.3.7.1 (Ulpian); Code Just. 5.12.6 (Maximian); Dig. Just. 24.3. (Ulpian); Dig. Just. 24.3.7.1–3 (Ulpian); Code Just. 5.12.29 (Justinian).

[154] Dig. Just. 9.2.27.30 (Ulpian); Dig. Just. 9.2.56 (Paul).

[155] Dig. Just. 24.1.44 (Neratius); Dig. Just. 24.1.40 (Ulpian); Dig. Just. 24.1.41 (Licinius Rufinus); Dig. Just. 24.1.42 (Gaius).

[156] Code Just. 5.9.6 (Leo and Anthemius).

[157] Dig. Just. 27.10.4 (Ulpian); Dig. Just. 37.15.1.pr–3 (Ulpian).

A. Origin of Paternal Power

326. I. Immediate origin. Marriage.[158]

327. II. Mediated origin. Adoption. Concept of this. Kinds, arrogation (*Arrogation*), and adoption in the narrow sense – adoptio minus plena. Arrogatio of an impubes. Prerequisites for the parties concerned. Effects of adoption.[159]

328. III. Unity of immediate and mediated origin. Legitimation. Concept and kinds of this. Legitimatio per subsequens matrimonium. Legitimatio per Curiae dationem. Legitimatio per rescriptum Principis. Relation of these kinds to one another. Effects of legitimation.

B. Legal Relations of Paternal Power

329. Relative status of children to the father. Former situation. Limitation [or reduction]. On the unitas personae.[160] Interdictum de liberis exhibendis.

330. Relative status of children to the father as regards economic relations. The child acquires from the father.

331. Exceptions to these rules. On the administration of children – peculium profectitium.

332. On the obligatory relations of paternal power – actio quod jussu – actio de peculio – actio tributoria – actio de in rem verso.

333. On the peculium castrense and quasi castrense.[161]

334. On the peculium adventitium. Its historical development. Rights of the father and son – peculium adventitium regulare and irregulare.[162]

335. On the legal remedies as regards maintaining and opposing paternal power.

C. Termination of Paternal Power

336. Natural dissolution. Death. Civil death.

337. Dissolution by elevation above the standpoint of the family. High office.

338. Cancellation of family bonds. Emancipation. Prerequisites and forms of this. Emancipatio Anastasiana. Emancipatio Justinianea. Effects of emancipation.

---

158 Dig. Just. 2.4.5 (Paul).

159 Dig. Just. 1.7.5 (Celsus); Dig. Just. 1.7.17.3–5 (Ulpian); Dig. Just. 5.2.29.3 (Ulpian); Code Just. 8.48.5 (Diocletian and Maximian).

160 Dig. Just. 43.30.1.5 (Ulpian).

161 Dig. Just. 49.17.2 (Ulpian).

162 Inst. Just. 2.9.1–2.

339. Cancellation as penalty.

340. Transition from paternal power to the separation of the family into families. Kinship.

341. Relation of agnation and cognation in Roman Law. The extent to which both later coincide.[163]

342. On kinship and its degrees. Descending line. Ascending line. Collateral line. Definitions of Roman and Canon Law. Multiple kinship relationships.

343. On affinity [relationship by marriage] according to Roman and Canon Law.

344. Dissolution of the family – capitis deminutio.[164]

345. The members of the family come to be *independent*, yet in such a way that they still need a *safeguard* for this *independence. Guardianship* [Tutel], *trusteeship* [Curatel].

Third Chapter: On Guardianship (Vormundschaft)

346. On guardianship (*Tutel*) as the completion of a foreign independence. On guardianship as family law. On guardianship as duty. On the altered position which guardianship is received [accepted] by us.[165]

347. On the difference between guardianship [Tutela] and trusteeship (*Cura*) – auctoritas and gestio.[166] Roman law. Present-day law.

348. On the kinds of tutela and cura.

A. Appointment of Guardianship (Vormundschaft)

349. On the capacity to be a guardian (*Vormund*). Exceptions.

350. On the obligation of guardianship. Excusing circumstances (*Excusationes*) against all guardianship as well as against specific guardianships.

351. On the grounds of denunciation for tutela as well as cura. Relationship to the law of succession. Tutela testamentaria. Tutela legitima. Tutela dativa. Duty of a tutor to entreat.[167]

352. On the appointment of guardian. Security. Swearing in. Roman law. Imperial laws.

---

163 Dig. Just. 50.16.195.2–5 (Ulpian).

164 Dig. Just. 4.5.11 (Paul).

165 Dig. Just. 26.1.1.pr–1 (Paul).

166 Dig. Just. 26.7.1.2–3 (Ulpian).

167 Dig. Just. 26.2.7 (Paul); Dig. Just. 26.2.9 (Pomponius); Dig. Just. 26.2.10.pr–1 (Ulpian); Dig. Just. 26.6.2.1–2 (Modestinus).

B. Legal Relations of Guardianship (Vormundschaft)

353. Relation of the guardian (*Vormundes*) to the ward. With respect to the person. With respect to the assets in its diverse connections. Difference between tutela and cura in this regard.[168]

354. On the joint administration of multiple guardians. On the variety of guardians in relation to management – gerentes – honorarii – notitiae causa dati. Their rights and duties. Relation to one another.[169]

355. On tutors (*Protutoren*) in relation to pupils and third persons – falsus tutor.[170]

356. On Nominatoren and Affirmatoren. Citizens.

357. On higher guardianship (*Obervormundschaft*). Duties of the higher guardian – partly direct in relation to the ward, partly indirect, in relation to the supervision of the guardian.[171]

358. On the legal remedies of the guardian and ward [person subject to curatorship]. Actio tutelae directa. Actio tutelae contraria. Actio de rationibus distrahendis.

C. Termination of Guardianship (Vormundschaft)

359. Cessation of the grounds of the guardianship. Death – capitis deminutio. Attaining age of majority.

360. Cancellation of guardianship. Resignation. Removal and dismissal of tutor suspectus. Process for it.[172]

361. Guardianship in its protection preserves the family in its dissolution. The complete dissolution of the family in the sphere of assets fulfills itself in the *law of succession.*

362. Transition to the law of succession.

Fifth Book: On the Law of Succession – Historical Introduction

First Chapter: On the Concept of the Roman Law of Succession

363. Principle of the Roman law of succession. Antithesis (*Grundsatz*) of testamentary and intestate succession – nemo pro parte testatus, pro parte intestatus decedere potest.

---

168 Dig. Just. 26.7.12.3–4 (Paul); Dig. Just. 26.7.15 (Paul); Dig. Just. 27.9.1.pr–4 (Ulpian).

169 Dig. Just. 26.7.53 (Paul); Code Just. 5.40.2 (Constantine).

170 Dig. Just. 27.5.1.pr–7 (Ulpian); Dig. Just. 47.2.54(53).3 (Paul).

171 Code Just. 5.32.1 (Antoninus); Code Just. 5.37.25 (Justinian).

172 Dig. Just. 26.10.8 (Ulpian); Dig. Just. 26.10.5 (Ulpian); Dig. Just. 26.10.9 (Modestinus).

364. On the meaning of this thesis. The variety of opinions about it.[173]

365. Exceptions to this principle. How they are justified.[174]

366. The Roman law of succession is thus subdivided essentially into intestate succession on one side and into testamentary succession on the other side. These are mutually related.

Second Chapter: On the Relation of Testamentary Succession to Intestate Succession

367. On testamentary succession. On intestate succession. On the union of both in compulsory right of inheritance (*Notherbenrecht*).

368. On wills calatis comitiis and procinctu. Different opinions about them. True meaning of this will. Unity of testamentary and intestate succession. Adoptive relationship. Proof of it.

369. On the pronouncement of the Twelve Tables, uti legassit etc. Separation of testamentary and intestate systems – testamentum per aes et libram. Diverse explanations of these.[175] True meaning.

370. On the effect of the antithesis of the testamentary and intestate systems. The will *ignores* [makes no provision for] the family. Pretermitting (*Praeterition*). The right to pretermit is disputed. *Necessary disinheritance* (*Nothwendige Exheredation*).

371. Who [is it that] must be disinherited? Method of disinheritance. Effects of pretermission.[176] On the bona mente exheredatio.[177]

372. On the relation of disinheritance to the institution. Conditions. Degrees.[178]

373. On the bonorum possessio contra tabulas. Relation to intestate succession. Who can petition for it. Effects of bonorum possessio contra tabulas.

374. On the bonorum possesio secundum tabulas. Relation to the testamentum per aes et libram.

375. The necessity of disinheritance expresses only a formal consideration for the family and not a consideration that has content. Lawsuits over it. Centumviri, quadruplex judicium. Querela inofficiosi testamenti. Meaning of the Querel.

376. The querela inofficiosi testamenti has even broader definitions – it includes the entire relation of blood kinship – it is only a subsidiary and

---

173 Cicero, *De Inventione Rhetorica* 2.21; Dig. Just. 50.17.7 (Pomponius); Dig. Just. 29.1.19 [?] (Ulpian); Dig. Just. 29.1.37 (Paul); Dig. Just. 29.2.39 (Ulpian); Dig. Just. 5.2.15.2 (Papinian).

174 Dig. Just. 49.17.19.2 (Tryphoninus).

175 Commentaries of Gaius 2.102; Dig. Just. 50.16.120 (Pomponius).

176 Dig. Just. 28.2.23 (Papinian); Dig. Just. 28.2.29.pr–1 (Scaevola).

177 Dig. Just. 28.2.18 (Ulpian); Dig. Just. 38.2.47.pr (Paul).

178 Code Just. 6.28.1 (Antoninus).

personal remedy outside of the system of law. Construction into a system of law. Presumptive insanity of the testator.[179]

377. On the effects of the querela inofficiosi testamenti. Abolition of the Querel – successio in querelam.

378. The Querel [considered] more precisely with reference to the quantity of the estate. *Forced share.*

379. On the forced share. Origin. Amount. Calculation. Manner of the bequest – querela inofficiosae donationis. Form of the bequest.

380. The Querel considered more precisely with reference to the persons entitled. Descendants. Ascendants. Siblings. Order of entitlements.[180]

381. It makes no difference whether the forced share has been bequeathed in part or omitted altogether – actio ad supplementum legitimae. Its consequence.

382. Present relationship of the intestate system to the testamentary system. Intestate succession should not merely preserve a fixed portion; it should itself be a system of testate succession. Novels 115. Its meaning.

383. Novels 115 is to be considered from three sides. I. Comparable treatment of disinheritance and pretermission. II. Grounds for excluding from intestate succession. Fixed specifications of them. III. Necessity of testamentary appointment.

384. Effects where Novels 115 is deficient. Inofficial system of citation. System of complete invalidity. System of mixed [or partial] invalidity.

385. The querela inofficiosi testamenti is still valid with respect to siblings. General survey of the relation of intestate succession to testamentary succession. Transition to the system of the will.

Third Chapter: On the Testamentary System, or on Wills, Legacies, Testamentary Trusts, and Gifts Causa Mortis

386. Concept of the will. Abstract freedom of choice. Sanctity of the will.[181]

387. On the testating subject. Who may make a will. *Mental impediments.* Being of unsound mind. Awareness of self proper. Familial impediments, filiifamilias, impuberes, spendthrift. Impediments that proceed from civil society.[182]

---

179 Dig. Just. 5.2.1 (Ulpian); Dig. Just. 5.2.8.15 (Ulpian); Dig. Just. 5.2.2 (Marcian); Dig. Just. 5.2.5 (Marcellus).

180 Code Just. 3.28.27 (Constantine).

181 Dig. Just. 28.1.1 (Modestinus); Dig. Just. 29.3.5 (Paul); Code Just. 1.2.1 (Constantine).

182 Dig. Just. 28.1.2 (Labeo); Dig. Just. 28.1.14 (Paul); Dig. Just. 28.1.15 (Ulpian); Dig. Just. 28.1.6.pr (Gaius).

388. A will requires the testator's *own* will – testamentum ex alieno arbitrio. Fair estimations of the third [rights of third persons?].[183]

389. A will requires *free* will. Influence of mistake, fraud, and coercion on a will. On the Senatusconsultum Libonianum. Dispositions to captators (*Captatorische Dispositionen*).[184]

390. On the conditions of the last will (*letzwilliger Verfügungen*) – poenae nomine legata – dies – modus.

391. On forms of wills. Ordinary form of will – testamentum principi ablatum. Judicial will. Extraordinary [nuncupative] form of wills. Will of a blind person. Will of a farmer on the land. Will [in the case of] infectious disease. Will of parents among children. Military will. Meaning of these.[185]

392. On the *manifestation* of the testator's will.

393. On the content of the will. With respect to assets, *as*. With respect to the designation of the devisees or legatees. Which persons may not be included as devisees or legatees? A devisee or legatee must be so voluntarily. Transition to substitution.

394. On common substitution. Concept. Its requirements and effects.

395. On substitution of a ward. Its double character. Effects and extinguishment. Quasi-pupillary substitution – precaria substitutio – entailed family estate.[186]

396. The progress and end of testamentary succession lies in substitution. Conflict of testamentary law of succession and bequest.

397. On the relation of the estate of the deceased to the bequest, and of the heirs to the legatees. Lex Furia. Lex Voconia. Lex Falcidia. Their calculation. Exceptions.

398. On the kinds of legacies – legatum vindicationis, praeceptionis – legatum damnationis. Union of both in legatum sinendi modo, Senatusconsultum Neronianum and in the Justinian ordinances.

399. Who can make a legacy? On the objects and concern of the legacy. Difference of legacy from inheritance in this respect. Legatum ususfructus. Servitudes, liens – nomen legatum – legatum debiti – liberatio legat – legatum dotis – annua legata – alimenta legata – legatum generis. Legacy of a Factum (*Factums*). Legacy of a universitas rerum. Legacy of something not one's own. Legacy of a quantity.

400. On the concept of legatum partitionis.

---

[183] Dig. Just. 28.5.32 (Gaius); Dig. Just. 28.5.69(68) (Pomponius); Dig. Just. 31.1.pr (Ulpian); Dig. Just. 30.75.pr (Ulpian).

[184] Dig. Just. 29.6.3 (Papinian); Dig. Just. 28.5.71(70) (Papinian); Dig. Just. 28.5.72(71) (Paul).

[185] Dig. Just. 29.1.1.pr (Ulpian).

[186] Dig. Just. 5.2.8.5 (Ulpian).

401. On the person of the legatarius. Preferential legacy[187] – a legatario legari non potest.

402. On the acquisition of the legacy – quando dies cedit – quando dies venit – agnition [Agnition]. Effects of acquisition. What can the legatee demand? What can be demanded in turn of the legatee? Legal remedies. Transition to the entailed estate.

403. Concept and origin of the entailed estate. Relation to the legacy and inheritance. Universal entailed estate. Singular entailed estate. Comparison of singular entailed estate and legacy. On the gift causa mortis – mortis causa captio.[188]

404. On the connections of universal entailed estates to the inheritance, and the meaning of S.C. Trebellianum and Pegasianum – Justinian's settlement.[189]

405. Of the relations of the tenant in possession of the entailed estate and the fiduciary.

406. On the form of bequests. Codicils (*Codicille*) – fideicommissum heredi praesenti injunctum. Codicillarclausel – regula Catoniana.[190]

407. On retraction of last wills – testamentum ruptum, irritum, destitutum.

408. On the revocation of the designation of beneficiary. Expiration of ten years, and retraction before three witnesses or before court. Destruction and withdrawal of the will. Later will.

409. On ademption and substitution (*Translation*) of a specific bequest.[191]

Fourth Chapter: On Intestate Succession

410. Principle of intestate succession.[192]

411. On intestate succession according to older civil law. Three classes – sui heredes – agnates – gentilen.[193]

412. On praetorian intestate succession. Supplementing a prior deficiency. Classe unde liberi. Classe unde legitimi. Classe unde cognati. Classe unde vir et uxor.

413. On the Edictum successorium.

414. On the changes of intestate succession up till Novels 118. Senatusconsultum Tertullianum. Orphitianum. Other imperial ordinances.

---

187 Dig. Just. 30.116.1 (Florentinus).
188 Inst. Just. 2.23.pr–2.
189 Inst. Just. 2.23.7.
190 Inst. Just. 2.25.pr.
191 Dig. Just. 34.4.6 (Paul).
192 Dig. Just. 38.6.1.pr (Ulpian).
193 Dig. Just. 48.20.7.pr (Paul); Dig. Just. 28.2.11 (Paul).

415. On intestate succession according to Novels 118. Principle of Novels 118 in contrast to prior law.[194] On the four classes of Novels 118.

416. First class – succession of descendants.

417. Second class – succession of ascendants, siblings of the full-blood and their children.[195]

418. Third class – succession of siblings of the half-blood and their children.

419. Fourth class – succession of other relatives according to the proximity of degree of kinship.

420. On multiple relationships [persons related in more than one way].

421. On the right of succession of spouses. Right of succession of the indigent widow.

422. Succession of children of concubines and their mothers.

423. On the right of succession to assets of freedmen [manumitted slaves]. Twelve Tables. Praetorian law and Lex Papia. Imperial constitutions. Succession of a libertus Latinus and dedititius.

424. On intestate succession which does not rest on kinship. Right of succession of the caretaker of a mentally incompetent person. Right of succession of certain colleagues [Collegia] – socius liberalitatis imperialis.[196]

425. On the right of succession of the state treasury.[197]

426. On the relation of intestate succession to the family in general survey [or summary]. Transition to the decedent's estate.

Fifth Chapter: The Doctrine of Heirship (Hereditas)

427. On heirs and on the inheritance. Relation of the heir to the inheritance. Place of the doctrine of inheritance in Roman Law.[198]

428. The heir and the inheritance are still separated – hereditas jacens.[199]

429. I. On the immediate relation of the heir to the inheritance – jus accrescendi [right to survival or accrual] – collatio.

430. On the right of survivorship. Concept of this. Right of survivorship of heirs by intestate succession. Right of survivorship of testamentary heirs –

---

194 Novels 118.5.

195 Novels 118.3.

196 Code Just. 10.14.1 (Constantine).

197 Code Just. 10.10.4 (Honorius and Theodosius).

198 Dig. Just. 28.5.35.pr (Ulpian); Dig. Just. 29.2.37 (Pomponius); Dig. Just. 50.16.208 (Africanus).

199 Dig. Just. 41.1.34 (Ulpian); Dig. Just. 41.1.61 (Hermogenianus).

re conjunctio – verbis conjunctio – re et verbis conjunctio. Right of survival of legatees.[200]

431. On the bringing together of descendants. Its purpose [*Prinzip*] and history. On the objects and the manner of collation. Decline of duty to bring together.[201]

432. II. On the mediated relation of heirs to the inheritance. Acquisition of the inheritance – sui et necessarii, extranei heredes – jus abstinendi.

433. On entering into the inheritance – cretio – pro herede gestio – nuda voluntas – jus deliberandi – beneficium inventarii. Agnition [?] of bonorum possessio. Effects of entering into the inheritance.

434. On the relation of the heir to joint heirs and others – actio familiae erciscundae – hereditatis petitio – interdictum quorum bonorum – remedium ex lege ult. C. de edicto Divi Hadriani tollendo.

435. III. On the renunciation of inheritance – transmissio. Indignity – hereditas vendita.

436. On the *transmissio* of inheritance – transmissio Theodosiana – transmissio Justinianea.

437. Loss of inheritance on account of indignity.

438. On the sale of inheritance.

Sixth Chapter: On Bonorum Possessio in Opposition to Hereditas

439. Origin of bonorum possessio. Difference from hereditas – bonorum possessio contra tabulas – bonorum possessio secundum tabulas – bonorum possessio intestati.

440. On extraordinary bonorum possessiones.

441. On the relation of bonorum possessio to hereditas – bonorum possessio cum re, sine re. The varieties of delation based on this. Significance today.

[200] Dig. Just. 29.2.35 (Ulpian); Dig. Just. 29.2.83 (Ulpian); Dig. Just. 28.5.60(59).2 (Celsus); Dig. Just. 28.5.67(66) (Pomponius); Dig. Just. 28.5.64(63) (Javolenus); Dig. Just. 28.5.17.1 (Ulpian); Code Just. 6.51.10 (Justinian).

[201] Dig. Just. 37.6.1 [Ulpian].

CHAPTER 3

GANS'S PREFACE TO HEGEL'S *PHILOSOPHY OF LAW* (1833)

Translator's note: All endnotes have been added by the translator.

The extraordinary gap that has arisen between the true value of the present book, on the one hand, and its recognition and acceptance by the public, on the other hand, impels me to touch on the issue in this enlarged edition. I would have preferred to leave this point to the progress of philosophical thinking. And I do not mean to address these comments either to the group which has long applied itself so earnestly to science. Nor do I mean to address that honorable group that feels drawn directly and instinctively rather than by pure consciousness to the grand form of the Hegelian system – a group that gladly and willingly subsists in the orbit of Hegel's system without bothering further with it.

The value of Hegel's Philosophy of Law, which is now published for the second time, does not consist so much in its argument and foundation, which were previously established by Rousseau and Kant by the end of the last century. Hegel did, of course, render those arguments and foundations deeper and firmer through the relentless energy that distinguished our friend above all else. But the value of his Philosophy of Law consists most of all in the execution, arrangement, and completely amazing architectonic that appears in every side and facet. Its value consists in the diligent effort that was applied to every nook and cranny of its edifice; and this value can be seen also in its style which is symmetrical and yet varied from its summit to foundation. The edifice as a whole surpasses all those medieval structures that were erected on restricted and narrow sites – older structures that detracted by their grandeur from their surroundings and nevertheless learned to conform taste to their heights. Has the German mind not laid a foundation for everything – or tried to? Shovel and spade always lie near to our hand, and we draft construction plans, while leaving the execution to grandchildren who no longer think about them. But it is rare for ideas that eschew abstraction to actually take shape, and it is still rarer for the tireless German mind to achieve with its realization a fresh beginning and larger circuit.

Another no less important value of the present Philosophy of Law consists in its decisive cancellation[209] of the distinction between state law and politics that was made by the abstract thought of the seventeenth and eighteenth centuries. Today many people still consider state law – whether positive or natural law – as the anatomical skeleton of the forms of the state from which life and motion have been drained. They try to apprehend the life that was once present by touching the lifeless forms and trying to recall some memory of the life. In opposition to state law, they call politics the more dynamic state science; this dynamic science embraces the operation of life in the individual parts and acquires a more or less arbitrary form according to the vital energies of the state. They see politics as the physiology of the state, so to speak. Such classifications and distinctions were unknown to antiquity: for antiquity there was but *one* whole, with *one* universality. The Republic of Plato and the Politics of Aristotle are at the same time both natural law and politics; they combine doctrines together with process of vital elaboration of the doctrines. For when the state is the whole life of freedom and what is external to the state appears only as barbarian, such distinctions could exist only internally and not as particular parts and ways of thinking. Such individual differences and abstractions rose to prominence only with the first rough application of theory during the emergence of the state from the particularism of the middle ages in the seventeenth and eighteenth centuries. With this, the dynamic movement that rested primarily on historical grounds became fundamentally separated from the science of practical statesmanship, and the Jurists inherited only their lifeless remnants. The modern state, however, is concerned with what has universal significance and interest, and it returns to the perspective of antiquity, albeit enriched by a thousand years of history. The modern state expresses the actuality of the customary idea which manifests itself in the form of customary spirit, and the modern state contains and preserves everything that appeared only abstractly and detached before it arose. The modern state must apprehend all distinctions as being only its own internal parts and not as something that affects it externally, and the state tries to put back together again and to develop into an organic whole what was separated by the past centuries. Consequently, nothing is left out of the present book that bears any relation to the state. Political questions are treated in detail, and even the science of rational economics is given its due place in the treatment of civil society.

A third great value of the current book – perhaps its most important – is the way that it establishes natural law not merely as a starting point and foundation for a science that goes before it; but rather it also establishes natural law as a result that flows over into a science that comes after it. Natural law theorists previously ignored the fact that natural law does not simply end but that it ends in something. They ignored the fact that just as natural law proceeds from the ground of subjective spirit, it likewise falls back into the currents of world history. Natural law must accordingly be approached as a mediate and connected science, a self-determined and progressing end, not an end severed from others. And what an awesome spectacle concludes this book. From the summit of the state, individual states are surveyed as just so many rivers flowing into the sea of world history, and the short sketch given of the development of world history does no more than suggest the more important topics that belong to that field.

Yet notwithstanding all the positive features of the book – the bedrock foundation that lies under its edifice, its wealth of style – it has come to pass through misunderstanding and false interpretation that this book has not only been estranged and concealed from the German public, but this book has actually been called a slavish work. And it has been asserted that every freedom loving man must keep his distance from its doctrines and basic principles. This state of affairs has come about not by any recourse to the book's contents (which would be equally false); rather it is mainly the result of harping on one single sentence of the Preface: "*What is rational is actual and what is actual is rational.*"[210] This sentence, which can actually be plainly interpreted, never meant to say, as Hegel's critics would have it, that the truly rational must, according to its nature, always be imagined as existing in the world at the present. Nor does it suggest that those things that truly exist in the world thus justify their own rationality. This sentence has now been taken up with great alarm and produced in order to deter readers from entering the book and reading its contents. It follows that, to be internally consistent, most of the detractors never bothered themselves with what else the work contains, for the sentence in question sufficed to frighten them off from any further reading or effort. The sentence kept them from making any closer approach and had the same effect as if the words inscribed over the entrance to Dante's hell were written over Hegel's book: *Lasciate ogni speranz, voi ch'entrate.*[211] And yet what did the reader find who, disregarding the widespread warning, actually drew near and went in? Did the reader not find the whole work constructed out of the material of freedom? Did he find some resisting force, some retrogressive homage in contemporary relationships to the middle ages, or some treatment of time perhaps as the source of disagreeable change? To mention only a few examples, did the author in a difficult time not set forth open judicial proceedings, open assembly meetings, and trials by jury as the only institutions appropriate to rationality? Did he comprehend monarchs as something besides the necessary and intellectually suitable summit of the state? Did he consider them merely the product of contingent historical circumstance? In speaking of freedom not merely as a constituent element of this book but rather its actual fabric, we do not mean that subjectively-loud freedom, that freedom that shoots up enthusiastically like a rocket. On the contrary, we mean freedom that saturates the fabric and contributes even greater solidity [to the work]. It is often the case with freedom that when it does not appear as opposed to something,[212] it is not deemed to be present. But the Hegelian theory[213] achieved a complete transformation; it transposed everything subjective into essential being, and consequently even incidental remarks achieved solidity.[214] Whoever reads Hegel's book without fear and studies it could not remain in doubt about its contents. For me this book first gave the courage to propose a new perspective for the science of law. And as one who has always cherished both freedom and science, revising this work has provided nothing but the most invigorating enjoyment and the still firmer confirmation of all my previous opinions of it.

Should I now mention the opponents not merely of the philosophy of law but rather of the whole philosophical standpoint from which it proceeds? All of us who have devoted ourselves to modern philosophy to enrich our special sciences or to raise them to a higher level have never uttered the name of *Schelling* except with the deepest respect. For us he ranks beside Plato and Aristotle, Descartes and Spinoza, Kant and Fichte. For us he is the youthful discoverer of the standpoint of modern philosophy, a Columbus who stands upon the islands and shore of a new world, but the interior of which is left to others to conquer. As so often happens, those who have made a great discovery directly in their minds no longer possess sufficient strength to accomplish its execution and completion; so the logical development of the philosophy of Schelling – and the dialectical method which regulates this development – has changed his philosophy into something else which, though it lacks Schelling's facility for writing down [philosophical insights], nevertheless possesses the more steadfast perseverance of the adult and spreads its substantial strength over the whole realm of the world. Of course, it is only natural and human to account for the retreat from progress for more than twenty-five years that also demonstrated [Schelling] to be essentially surpassed, and to struggle against it as against logical fetters that threaten to destroy freedom and life. But it is harder to account for the fact that the great founder of Identity Philosophy could depart so completely his earlier character and abandon his principles by seeking sanctuary in scientifically impenetrable faith and history. His new philosophy, newly retitled "*Historical*," has subordinated itself to and proven its dependence upon history. Should it be the case, as it nearly seems to be, that the Historical School of Jurisprudence were drawn into the orbit of Schelling's philosophy, then this school would achieve the honor of coming to be a philosophy, without knowing how. But to those who labor to achieve this end, we have the following to say. As soon as they have entered the system of logical philosophy they are offended that they cannot at the same time also remain outside [the system]; they complain about the fetters which are, or should be, however, just the reason of the thing; [and] they would rather keep to the arbitrary methods to which they are accustomed and to be able to think, sing, and pray. They would like to grasp God, but they fear to approach him too closely, and they are seized with fear by the prospect of the hazardous undertaking. They want to retain *along side* philosophy the consolation that is *external to* philosophy, and for all that, they also want the last word *over* philosophy. But systems can be displaced only by systems, and as long as they do not offer to prepare a scientific [system] for us, we must stay with the one that we have.

I now turn to the main questions about the methods and basic principles adopted in the preparation of the present text of Natural Law. *Hegel* lectured three times on his compendium in the winter semesters of 1821–22, 1822–23, and 1824–25.[215] When he resumed teaching this course in the winter of 1831, he was overtaken by death after only a few lectures. From this it appears that the lectures were in part delivered soon after the original publication of the book and in part later broken off – not to the extent usual for Hegel with other objects where there was an expansion of substantive coverage, a broader perspective, and a change in classifications. The actual advantage which the general public derives from lectures over a book lies in their presentation in a easier manner that is closer to the usual style of common understanding. Nevertheless, there is a serious difficulty with bringing the lectures together with the text of the book in a way that avoids having the heterogenous character of either lectures or book appear too strikingly. If the book is taken as foundation, one can certainly not include everything from the lectures, because they repeat parts of the book, albeit pulverized and otherwise prepared; and reproducing the lectures would have made even more frequent repetitions unavoidable. It is thus necessary to sift through the existing material and take its core which, even if it contains nothing really new, still contains something that helps illuminate and explain the contents. Here these selections from the lectures are given in the form of additions, which number almost 200 in this edition. These additions often explain the contents of the main paragraphs by providing examples; they often say the same thing, only more clearly and in more popular language; and they even more often facilitate the communication of ideas to the common consciousness. The solidity found in the book in general is thus made even more solid, and a breach is introduced into the fabric that is difficult and hard to penetrate; and through this breach a large number of persons who were previously excluded can make their entrance. The substance of the additions derives from Hegel, and I can prove this if necessary from my sources. The additions are neither my exposition nor a misstatement of the material from which they are taken. I have adjusted only the stylistic arrangement, the connection of sentences, and, on occasion, the choice of words. This revised edition is based chiefly on two student notebooks. One from the winter semester of 1822–23 was transcribed by my friend *Hotho*; the other from the half-year 1824–25 was transcribed by Captain von *Griesheim*. Unfortunately, this revised edition has the pleasure less often of referring to Hegel's own interleaved manuscript notes in his copy of the Philosophy of Law. Such cases were limited for the most part to individual words that were not clear from the context and that could be interpreted ambiguously or falsely. When Hegel's notes were consulted, they proved extremely helpful.

In presenting this book to the public with an accurate account of its origin, it remains for me only to mention its future prospects. As part of the Hegelian system, the book will rise or fall with that system. It will also, perhaps, be susceptible of more cogent elucidation, more sophisticated elaboration, and greater specificity. Perhaps, like the system as a whole, it will pass over after many years into imaginative thought and become part of the universal consciousness: if so, it will lose its characteristic technical terminology, and its deepest recesses will become common property. Then its time is philosophically over, and it belongs to history. A new and different interpretation of actuality, which has itself altered, comes forth out of the same basic principles from the foregoing progressive development of philosophy. We purpose to welcome this future with respect; and let us not, on the contrary, be apprehensive of specters of the departed which may affect us disagreeably but cannot hinder us.

Berlin, May 29, 1833
Eduard Gans

CHAPTER 4

GLOSSARY[216]

Actio. Cause of action. Actio famosa. Cause of action for certain wrongful conduct that resulted in infamia. Actio in factum and actio utilis were causes of action for remedies that were provided by the praetor that supplemented or amplified remedies available under the civil law proper.

Arrha. (From Hebrew). Earnest money or money given to ratify a contract. (Part of the contract price as opposed to pignus, which is a sum of money, given as security, that is returned when the contract is performed.)

Bonorum possessio. The right of possession of an estate recognized by the praetor. The praetor developed rules of succession that diverged from the civil law rules of testate and intestate succession, and the praetorian law ultimately prevailed because of the superior remedies it provided. The two systems were merged under Justinian.

Captator. Literally, one who strives for something. Applied to one who searches for legacies. *Cf.* gold digger.

Codicilli. Codicil or appendix supplementing or amending a will.

Cura. Legal guardianship by a guardian (Curator) over insane persons, spendthrifts, and certain minors.

Delation. Accusation or denunciation.

Delict. Civilian term for torts. It is used instead of torts, because the term torts (which acquired currency only in the nineteenth century) would be too shamefully anachronistic.

Emphyteusis. Contract for lease of real property to a tenant (the "emphyteuta").

Fideicommissum. Legal obligation imposed on an heir or legatee to transfer property. The German term *Fideikommis* is sometimes rendered as fee tail in contemporary legal use, but Gans employed the term as the vernacular for the Latin fideicommissum, which imposed a moral obligation upon the title holder to transfer to another. This moral obligation was made legally binding under Augustus. The sense of personal duty and the distinction between legal and moral obligation are better expressed by translating the term as "testamentary trust."

Gens. Gentilen. Form of succession by a member of an extended kinship group (gens).

Hereditas. Heirship, inheritance, succession to the legal interests of the deceased. Inheritance could be either testate or intestate but, in theory, had to be either completely one or the other. Such succession refers to the descent under the rules of the civil law as distinguished from the bonorum possessio administered by the praetor.

Infamia. Status of legal disability entailing public shame that resulted from criminal and delictual liability.

Legator. Testator of a legatum (legacy). See voluntas legatoria.

Legatum. Legacy. A bequest of something less than the entire estate and, therefore, considered a reduction of the inheritance.

Mensor. Surveyor of land. Roman Law established a cause of action against mensors for wrongful surveying.

Praetor. A magistrate with a mix of legislative and judicial powers. (The number and type changed.) The Praetor, by announcing rules that he would administer (in an edict), legislated a body of private law rules of decision that came to be known as the *jus honorarium*, as distinct from the *jus civile*. The cumulative valid provisions of such edicts came to called "the Edict." Much of the Digest comprised selections from the commentaries of the jurists on this Edict.

Querel [-a, or ella]. Complaint or accusation.

Servitus. Servitude or property-like right to use property of another in a certain way. It was a broad term that applied both to personal rights to use (usufruct) and rights of way, easements, and profits attached to land.

Superficies. The transfer of rights to build on the surface of real property. The term also refers to the building or improvements constructed on the surface.

Testament[um]. Testament, or legal act of publication of a last will or testament by a testator or testatrix. The chief validating event of such a testament was the appointment of an heir. The testament could contain legacies, testamentary trusts, and other legal dispositions.

Transmissio. General term for passing over, transferring, or transmitting. Applied to the passage of property to heirs or legatees.

Tutel[a]. Legal guardianship by a tutor (protutor) over a young minor.

Usufruct[us]. Property-like right to the use of property or the benefits, income, or crops produced by the property.

Voluntas legatoria. Legacy, last will.

CHAPTER 5

APPENDIX

GANS'S PREFACE TO *HEGEL'S PHILOSOPHY OF HISTORY* (1837)
TRANSLATED BY J. SIBREE (1857)

Editor's Note

Gans posthumously edited Hegel's lecture notes for courses on the philosophy of history and published them in book form as *The Philosophy of History* (1837). Karl Hegel significantly revised the text for a second edition (1840). Sibree translated the work in 1857, employing the Karl Hegel text. Sibree's work has been continuously in print in a variety of English and American editions ever since. Sibree's translation is arguably the most historically influential and successful translation of any of Hegel's works.

Sibree published translations of both Gans's and Karl Hegel's prefaces as Prefaces to the First and Second Edition, respectively. Although the Gans preface was reprinted repeatedly in nineteenth-century editions in both England and America, appearing as late as 1902 in the American Home Library edition – it was omitted from the Colonial Press edition of 1899 upon which the edition currently in print is based.[217]

The text below is copied from the first English (not American) edition.[218] Punctuation, spelling, and misspelling[219] have been retained. The text in brackets and all of the footnotes appeared in Sibree's original.

PREFACE TO THE FIRST EDITION

The first question that suggests itself on the publication of a new Philosophy of History is why, of all the departments of so-called Practical Philosophy, this should have been the latest cultivated and the least adequately discussed. For it was not until the beginning of the eighteenth century that *Vico* made the first attempt to substitute for that view of History which regarded it either as a succession of fortuitous occurrences, or as the supposed but not clearly recognized work of God, a conception of it as an embodiment of primordial laws, and a product of Reason – a theory which so far from contravening the moral freedom of humanity, posits the only conditions in which that freedom can be developed.

This fact can however be explained in a few brief observations. The laws of Being and Thought, the economy of Nature, the phenomena of the human soul, even legal and political organisms; nor less the forms of Art and the acknowledged manifestations of God in other modes have always passed for stable and immutable existences, if not as far as subjective views of them are concerned, yet certainly in their objective capacity. It is otherwise with the movements of History. The extrinsic contingency which predominates in the rise and fall of empires and of individuals, the triumphs of vice over virtue, the confession sometimes extorted, that there have been instances in which crimes have been productive of the greatest advantage to mankind, and that mutability, which must be regarded as the inseparable companion of human fortunes, tend to keep up the belief that History stands on such a basis of shifting caprice, on such an uncertain fire-vomiting volcano, that every endeavour to discover rules, ideas, the Divine and Eternal *here*, may be justly condemned as an attempt to insinuate adventitious subtleties, as the bubble-blowing of à priori construction, or a vain play of imagination. While men do not hesitate to admire God in the objects of Nature, it is deemed almost blasphemy to recognize him in human exertions and human achievements; it is supposed to be an exaltation of the disconnected results of caprice – results which a mere change of humour might have altered – above their proper value, to suppose a principle underlying them for which the passions of their authors left no room in their own minds. In short, men revolt from declaring the products of Free-Will and of the human spirit to be eternal, because they involve only *one* element of stability and consistency – the advance amid constant mutability to a richer and more fully developed character. An important advance in Thought was required, a filling up of the "wide gulf" that separates Necessity from Liberty, before a guiding hand could be demonstrated as well as recognized in this *most intractable* because most *unstable* element – before a Government of the World in the History of the World could be, not merely asserted but indicated, and Spirit be regarded as no more abandoned by God than Nature. Before this could be done, a series of millenniums must roll away: the work of the human spirit must reach a high degree of perfection, before that point of view can be attained, from which a comprehensive survey of its career is possible. Only now, when Christendom has elaborated an outward embodiment for its inward essence, in the form of civilized and free states, has the time arrived not merely for a History based on Philosophy, but for the Philosophy of History.

One other remark must not be withheld, and which is perhaps adapted to reconcile even the opponents of Philosophy, at least to convince them that in the ideal comprehension of History, the original facts are not designed to be altered or violence of any kind done them. The remark in question has reference to what is regarded as belonging to Philosophy in these events. Not every trifling occurrence, not every phenomenon pertaining rather to the sphere of individual life than to the course of the World-Spirit, is to be "construed," as it is called, and robbed of its life and substance by a withering formula. There is nothing more alien to intelligence, and consequently nothing more ridiculous than the descending to that micrology which attempts to explain indifferent matters – which endeavours to represent that as necessitated which might have been decided in one way quite as well as in another, and of which in either case, he who presumes to construe the occurrence in question, would have found an explanation. Philosophy is degraded by this mechanical application of its noblest organs, while a reconciliation with those who occupy themselves with its empirical details is thereby rendered impossible. What is left for Philosophy to claim as its own, consists not in the demonstration of the necessity of all occurrences, – in regard to which, on the contrary, it may content itself with mere narration, – but rather in removing that veil of obscurity which conceals the fact that every considerable aggregate of nations, every important stadium of History has an idea as its basis, and that all the transitions and developments which the annals of the past exhibit to us, can be referred to the events that preceded them. In this artistic union of the merely descriptive element on the one hand, with that which aspires to the dignity of speculation, on the other hand, will lie the real value of a Philosophy of History.

Again, the treatises on the Philosophy of History that have appeared within the last hundred years or thereabout differ in the point of view from which they have been composed, vary with the national character of their respective authors, and lastly, are often mere indications of a Philosophy of History than actual elaborations of it. For we must at the outset clearly distinguish *Philosophies* from *Theosophies*, which latter resolve all events directly into God, while the former unfold the manifestation of God in the real world. Moreover, it is evident that the Philosophies of History which have appeared among the Italians and the French, have but little connection with a general system of thought, as constituting one of its organic constituents; and that their views, though often correct and striking, cannot demonstrate their own inherent necessity. Lastly, much has often been introduced into the Philosophy of History that has been of a mystical, rhapsodical order, that has not risen above a mere fugitive hint, an undeveloped fundamental idea; and though in many cases the great merit of such contributions cannot be denied, their place would be only in the vestibule of our science. We have certainly no wish to deny that among the Germans, *Leibnitz*, *Lessing*, *Weguelin*, *Iselin*,

Kant, Fichte, Schelling, Schiller, W. von Humboldt,[1] *Görres, Steffens* and *Rosencranz,*[2] have given utterance to observations of a profound, ingenious and permanently valuable order, respecting both the basis of History generally and the connection that exists between events and the spirit of which they are demonstrably the embodiment. Among French writers, who would refuse to admire in *Bossuet* the refined ecclesiastical and teleological genius which regards the History of the World as a vast map spread out before it; in *Montesquieu* the prodigious talent that makes events transform themselves *instanter* to thoughts in his quick apprehension; or in *Balanche* and *Michelet* the seer's intuition that pierces the superficial crust of circumstances and discerns the hidden forces with which they originated? But if actually elaborated Philosophies of History are in question, four writers only present themselves, *Vico, Herder, Fr. v. Schlegel,*[3] and lastly the Philosopher whose work we are here introducing to the public.

Vico's life and literary labours carry us back to a period in which the elder philosophies are being supplanted by the Cartesian; but the latter has not yet advanced beyond the contemplation of the fundamental ideas – Being and Thought; it is not yet equipped for a descent into the concrete World of History, or prepared to master it. Vico, in attempting to exhibit the principles of History in his "Scienza Nuova," is obliged to rely on the guidance of the ancients and to adopt the classical [φιλοτοφηματα]: in his investigations it is the data of ancient rather than of modern records that arrest his attention: Feudality and its history is with him rather a supplement to the development of Greece and Rome than something specifically distinct therefrom. Although at the close of his book he asserts that the Christian religion, even in its influence on human aims, excels all the religions of the world, he stops short of anything like an elaboration of this statement. The separation and distinction between the Middle Ages and the Modern Time cannot be exhibited, as the Reformation and its effects are excluded from consideration. Besides, he undertakes to discuss the rudiments of human intelligence, Language, Poetry, Homer; as a Jurist he has to go down into the depths of Roman Law, and to investigate them; while all this – the main stream of thought, episodes, expansion of the ideas and reverting to their principles – is further varied by a proneness to hunt out etymologies and give verbal explanations, which often serves to retard and disturb the most important processes of historical evolution. Most persons are thus deterred by the repulsive exterior from apprehending the

[1] In an academic dissertation, whose style is as masterly as its contents are profound: "*On the Task of the Historian.*"

[2] In his animated and genially clever tractate: "*What the Germans have accomplished for the Philosophy of History.*"

[3] Translated in Bohn's Standard Library.

profound truths which it envelopes; the latter are not sufficiently obvious on the surface, and the gold is thrown away with the dross that conceals it.

In *Herder* we find traits of excellence which are wanting in Vico. He is himself a poet, and he approaches History in a poetic spirit; moreover he does not detain the reader by prefatory inquiries into the foundations and vestibules of History – Poetry, Art, Language, and Law: he begins immediately with points of climate and geography; moreover the entire field of History lies open before him: his liberal Protestant and cosmopolitan culture gives him an insight into all nationalities and views, and renders him capable of transcending mere traditional notions to an unlimited extent. Sometimes, too, he hits upon "the right word" with wonderful felicity; the teleological principle on which his speculations are based does not hinder him from doing justice to the varieties [of the actual world], and in comparing historical periods the analogy they bear to the stages of human life does not escape him. But these "Ideas contributory to the Philosophy of the History of Mankind" contradict their title by the very fact that not only are all metaphysical categories banished, but a positive hatred to metaphysics is the very element in which they move. The Philosophy of History in Herder's hands therefore, broken off from its proper basis, is a highly intellectual, often striking, and on the other hand often defective "*raisonnement*" – a Theodicaea rather of the Heart and Understanding than of Reason. This alienation from its natural root leads by necessary consequence to an enthusiasm which often obstructs the current of thought, and to interjections of astonishment, instead of that contention of mind which results in demonstration. The theologian, the genial preacher, the entranced admirer of the works of God, very often intrudes with his subjective peculiarities amid the objectivity of History.

In *Frederick v. Schlegel's* Philosophy of History we may find, if we choose to look, a fundamental idea, which can be called a philosophical one. It is this, namely, that Man was created free; that two courses lay before him, between which he was competent to choose – that which led upwards, and that which led downwards to the abyss. Had he remained firm and true to the primary will that proceeded from God, his freedom would have been that of blessed spirits; that view being rejected as quite erroneous, which represents the paradisaical condition as one of blissful idleness. But as man unhappily chose the second path, there was from that time forward a divine and a natural will in him; and the great problem for the life of the individual as also for that of the entire race, is the conversion and transformation of the lower earthly and natural will more and more into the higher and divine will. This Philosophy of History, therefore, really begins with the dire and strange lament, that there should be a history at all, and that man did not remain in the unhistorical condition of blessed spirits. History, in this view, is an apostasy – the obscuration of man's pure and divine being; and instead of a possibility of discovering God in it, it is rather the Negative of God which is mirrored in it. Whether the race will ultimately succeed in returning completely and entirely to God, is on this shewing only a matter of expectation and hope, which, since humanity has once more darkened its prospects by Protestantism, must, at least to Frederick v. Schlegel, appear doubtful. In elaborating the characteristic principles and historical development of the several nations, wherever that fundamental idea retires somewhat into the background, an intellectual platitude manifests itself, which seeks to make up by smooth and polished diction for the frequent tenuity of the thought. A desire to gain repose for his own mind, to justify himself, and to maintain the Catholic stand-point against the requirements of the modern world, gives his treatise a somewhat far-fetched and premeditated tone, which deprives facts of their real character to give them that tinge which will connect them with the results they are brought forward to establish.

Hegel's Lectures on the Philosophy of History, to which we now come, have at starting a great advantage over their predecessors, apart from the merits of their contents. First and foremost they are connected with a system of thought logically elaborated even to its minutest members: they claim to exhibit the Logos of History, just as there is a Logos of Nature, of the Soul, of Law, of Art, &c. Here, then, mere flashes of thought, mere "*raisonnement*," intelligent or unintelligent intuitions are out of the question; instead of these we have an investigation conducted by logical philosophy in the department of those human achievements [which constitute History]. The categories have been already demonstrated in other branches of the System, and the only point left to be determined is, whether they will be able also to verify themselves in the apparently intractable element of human caprice. But in order that this proceeding may bring with it a guarantee of its correctness, and I might also say, of its honesty, the occurrences themselves are not metamorphosed by Thought, exhibited as otherwise than they really are, or in any way altered. The facts remain as they were – as they appear in the historical traditions of centuries: the Idea is their expositor, not their perverter; and while the Philosophy of History thus involves nothing more than the comprehension of the hidden meaning of the outward phenomenon, the philosophical *art* will consist in perceiving in what part of these phenomenal data a ganglion of Ideas lies, which must be announced and demonstrated as such; and, as in Nature every straw, every animal, every stone cannot be deduced from general principles, so the art in question will also discern where it should rise to the full height of speculation, or where, as remarked above, it may be content to lose itself in the confines of the merely superficial; it will know what is demonstrable, and what is simply attached to the demonstration as portraiture and characteristics; conscious of its dignity and power, it will not be content to expend its labour on indifferent circumstances.

This is in fact one of the chief merits of the present Lectures, that with all the speculative vigour which they display, they nevertheless concede their due to the Empirical and Phenomenal; that they equally repudiate a subjective *raisonnement* [a discussion following the mere play of individual fancy,] and the forcing of all historical data into the mould of a formula; that they seize and present the Idea both in logical development and in the apparently loose and irregular course of historical narrative, but yet without allowing this process to appear obtrusively in the latter. The so-called *à priori* method – which is, in fact, presumed to consist in 'making up' history without the aid of historical facts – is therefore altogether different from what is presented here; the author had no intention to assume the character of a God, and to *create* History, but simply that of a man, addressing himself to consider that History which, replete with reason and rich with ideas, had already been created.

The character of Lectures gives the work an additional advantage, which it would perhaps have wanted had it been composed at the outset with a view to publication as a book, and with the compact energy and systematic seriousness which such a design would have involved. Consisting of lectures, it must contemplate an immediate apprehension of its 'meaning;' it must be intended to excite the interest of youthful hearers, and associate what is to be presented to their attention with what they already know. And as of all the materials that can be subjected to philosophic treatment, History is always the one with whose subject persons of comparatively youthful years become earliest acquainted, the *Philosophy* of History may also be expected to connect itself with what was previously known, and not teach the subject itself as well as the ideas it embodies (as is the case, *e.g.* in AEsthetics,) but rather confine itself to exhibiting the workings of the Idea in a material to which the hearer is supposed to be no stranger. If this be done in a method partly constructive, partly merely characteristic, the advantage will be secured of presenting to the student a readable work – one which has affinities with ordinary intelligence, or at least is not very much removed from it. These Lectures therefore – and the remark is made without fear of contradiction – would form the readiest introduction to the Hegelian Philosophy: they are even more adapted to the purpose than the "Philosophy of Right" [or Law,] which certainly presupposes in the student some ideas of its subject to begin with. But the advantages of the Lecture form are not unaccompanied by the usual drawbacks in the present case. The necessity of developing principles at the commencement, of embracing the entire subject, and of concluding within definite limits, must occasion an incongruity between the first and the latter part of the work. The opulence of facts which the Middle Ages offer us, and the wealth of ideas that characterizes the Modern Time, may possibly induce dissatisfaction at the attention which, simply because it is the beginning, is devoted to the East.

This naturally leads us to the principles which have been adopted in the composition of the work in its present dress; as they concern, first, its contents, and secondly, its form. In a lecture, the teacher endeavours to individualize his knowledge and acquisitions: by the momentum of oral delivery he breathes a life into his intellectual materials which a mere book cannot possess. Not only are digressions, amplifications, repetitions, and the introduction of analogies which are but distantly connected with the main subject, in place in every lecture, but without these ingredients an oral discourse would be dry and lifeless. That *Hegel* possessed this didactic gift, notwithstanding all prejudices to the contrary, might be proved by his manuscripts alone, which by no means contain the whole of what was actually delivered, as also by the numerous changes and transformations that mark the successive resumptions of an old course of lectures. The illustrations were not unfrequently disproportioned to the speculative matter; the beginning (and simply because it was such) was so greatly expanded, that if all the narrative sections, descriptions, and anecdotes had been inserted, essential detriment would have resulted to the appearance of the book. In the first delivery of his lectures on the Philosophy of History, Hegel devoted a full third of his time to the Introduction and to China – a part of the work which was elaborated with wearisome prolixity. Although in subsequent deliveries he was less circumstantial in regard to this Empire, the editor was obliged to reduce the description to such proportions as would prevent the Chinese section from encroaching upon, and consequently prejudicing the treatment of, the other parts of the work. That kind of editorial labour which was most called for in this part was necessary in a less degree in all the other divisions. The Editor had to present Lectures in the form of a Book: he was obliged to turn oral discourse into readable matter: the notes of students and the manuscripts which constituted his materials were of different dates; he had to undertake the task of abridging the diffuseness of delivery, bringing the narrative matter into harmony with the speculative observations of the author, taking due precautions that the later lectures should not be thrust into a corner by the earlier ones, and that the earlier ones should be freed from that aspect of isolation and disconnection which they presented. On the other hand, he was bound not to forget for one moment that the book contained lectures; the naïveté, the *abandon*, the enthusiastic absorption in the immediate subject which makes the speaker indifferent as to when or how he shall finish, had to be left intact; and even frequent repetitions, where they did not too much interrupt the course of thought, or weary the reader, could not be altogether obliterated.

But notwithstanding the full measure of license, which in the nature of the case must be conceded to the Editor, and the reconstructive duties imposed upon him by compilation, it can be honestly averred that in no case have the ideas of the compiler been substituted for those of Hegel, – that a genuine, altogether unadulterated work of the great philosopher is here offered to the reader, and that, if the editor had followed another plan, no choice would have been left him but either to produce a book which none could have enjoyed, or, on the other hand, to insert too much of his own in place of the materials that lay before him.

As regards the style of the work, it must be observed that the Editor was obliged to write it out from beginning to end. For one part of the Introduction, however, (as far as p. 61 of this book) he had ready to hand an elaboration begun by Hegel in 1830, which though it was not designed expressly for publication, was manifestly intended to take the place of earlier Introductions. The Editor – though all his friends did not adopt his view of the matter – believed that where a Hegelian torso was in existence, he ought to refrain from all interpolations of his own and from revisional alterations. He was desirous not to weaken the firm phalanx of the Hegelian style by introducing phrases of any other stamp or order, even at the risk of being thus obliged to forego a certain unity of expression. He thought that it could not be otherwise than gratifying to the reader to encounter – at least through some part of the book – the strong, pithy and sometimes gnarled style of the author; he wished to afford him the pleasure of pursuing the labyrinthine windings of thought under the guidance of his often less than flexible but always safe and energetic hand. From the point at which these elaborated fragments ceased, began the real task of giving the work an integral form; but this was performed with constant regard for the peculiar terms of expression which the manuscripts and notes exhibited: the Editor gladly exchanged the words which offered themselves to his own pen for others which he would perhaps not have preferred himself, but which seemed to him more characteristic of the author; only where it was absolutely necessary has he been willing to complete, to fill up, to supplement; in short he has been anxious as far as possible to make no sort of change in the peculiar type of the composition, and to offer to the public not a book of his own but that of another. The Editor cannot therefore become responsible for its expression, as if it were his own; he had to present a material and trains of thought not his own, and as far as possible to avoid travelling far out of the limits of that order of phrases in which they were originally clothed. Only within these given and predetermined conditions, which are at the same time impediments to a free style, can the Editor be made accountable.

Hegel's *manuscripts* were the first materials to which the Editor had recourse. These often contain only single words and names connected by dashes, evidently intended to aid the memory in teaching; then again longer sentences, and sometimes a page or more fully written out. From this latter part of the manuscript could be taken many a striking expression, many an energetic epithet: the hearers' notes were corrected and supplemented by it, and it is surprising with what unwearied perseverance the author continually returns to former trains of thought. Hegel appears in these memorials as the most diligent and careful teacher, always intent upon deepening fugitive impressions, and clenching what might pass away from the mind, with the strong rivets of the Idea. As regards the second part of my materials, the *notes*, I have had such – reporting all the five deliveries of this course, 1822/23, 1824/25, 1826/27, 1828/29, 1830/31[4] – in the hand-writing of Geh. Ober-Regierungs Rath Schulze, Capt. von Grieshein, Prof. Hotho, Dr. Werder, Dr. Heimann, and the son of the philosopher, M. Charles Hegel. It was not till the session of 1830/31 that Hegel came to treat somewhat more largely of the Middle Ages and the Modern Time, and the sections of the present work devoted to those periods are for the most part taken from this last delivery of the course. To many of my respected colleagues and friends, whom I would gladly name if I might presume upon their permission to do so, I am indebted for emendations, additions, and assistance of every kind. Without such aids, the book would be much less complete as regards the historical illustration of principles than it may perhaps be deemed at present.

With this publication of the "Philosophy of History," that of the "AEsthetik" within a few months, and that of the "Encyclopädie" in its new form and style, which will not have long to be waited for, the work of editing and publishing Hegel's writings will be completed. For our Friend and Teacher it will be a monument of fame; for the editors a memorial of piety, whose worth and truth consist not in womanish lamentation, but in a grief that is only a stimulus to renewed activity. On the other hand that piety desires no return but the satisfaction which it already possesses in the consciousness of the performance of duty; and though those who are "dead while they live" may think to reproach us with the feebleness of our means, we may hope for absolution in consideration of the plenitude of our zeal. The Hegelian Four Ages of the World have at least made their appearance.

EDUARD GANS.
Berlin, June 8, 1837.

[4] These lectures were delivered in the University of Berlin, to which Hegel was called in 1818. "He there lectured for thirteen years, and formed a school, of which it is sufficient to name as among its members, Gans, Rosenkranz, Michelet, Werder, Marheineke and Hotho." Lewes's Biog. Hist. of Philos. – TR.

NOTES

1. The group of leading Hegel scholars who edited Hegel's worksposthumously included:
   Gans (Professor of Law at Berlin)
   Marheineke (Professor of Theology at Berlin)
   Schulze (who held a variety of ministerial positions)
   Henning (Professor of Philosophy at Berlin)
   Hotho (Professor of Aesthetics at Berlin)
   Michelet (Professor of Philosophy at Berlin)
   Förster (Curator of the Berlin Museum).
   These scholars were all drawn to Hegel in the first two decades of the nineteenth century. Hegel referred to Gans in his letters more often than to any of the others.
2. A number of Gans's works have been recently republished in German. E.g., Norbert Waszek, ed., *Eduard Gans (1797–1839): Hegelianer-Jude-Europäer: Texte und Dokumente*, Hegeliana: Studien und Quellen an Hegel und zum Hegelianismus, ed. Helmut Schneider, vol. 1 (Frankfurt am Main: Peter Lang, 1991) (contains Gans's Autobiographical Notice, three Addresses to the Jewish Union, and several essays on political topics); Eduard Gans, *Naturrecht und Universalrechtsgeschichte*, ed. Manfred Riedel (Klett-Cotta, 1981) (transcribes notes to his lectures on natural law and universal history and polemical writings against the Historical School of jurisprudence); *Philosophische Schriften*, ed. Horst Schröder (Glashütten im Taunus: Detlev Auvermann, 1971) (transcribes notes to lectures on the philosophy of law and on German constitutional law, and reprinting miscellaneous reviews and prefaces); "Erwiderung auf Schubart (1839)," in *Materialien zu Hegels Rechtsphilosophie*, ed. Manfred Riedel, vol. 1 (Frankfurt am Main: Suhrkamp, 1975), 267–75. There is some duplication; for example, most of these titles reprint Gans's Preface to Hegel's *Philosophy of Law*; Gans's 1824 Preface to his multivolume *Law of Inheritance* is also included in each.
   The most complete list of recent scholarship on Gans is Waszek's bibliography in his edition of Eduard Gans, *Rückblicke auf Personen und Zustände*, new ed. (Bad Cannstadt: Frommann-Holzboog, 1994), 435–47.
3. Translations of Gans's work include the bylaws of the Society for the Culture and Science of the Jews (which he co-authored), trans. J. Hessing and P. Mendes-Flohr, in *The Jew in the Modern World: A Documentary History*, ed. Paul R. Mendes-Flohr and Jehuda Reinharz (New York: Oxford University Press, 1980), 188–89; and "A Society to Further Jewish Integration" [Gans's address to the Union for the Culture and Science of Jews of April 28, 1822], trans. J. Hessing, ibid., 190–93.
   For recent treatments of Gans in English, see Norbert Waszek, "Eduard Gans on Poverty: Between Hegel and Saint-Simon," *Owl of Minerva* 18 (1987): 167–78; and idem, "The Stagnation of the Consciousness of Freedom: A Challenge to Hegelianism," in *Denken Unterwegs: Philosophie im Kräftfeld sozialen und politischen Engagements*, Festschrift

für Heinz Kimmerle zu seinem 60. Geburtstag, ed. Henk Oosterling and Frans de Jong (Amsterdam: Verlag B.R. Grüner, 1990), 175–85.

The "Additions" that Gans published in his posthumous edition of Hegel's *Philosophy of Law* have been incorporated in most English translations. E.g., G.W.F. Hegel, *Elements of the Philosophy of Right*, ed. Allen W. Wood, trans. H.B. Nisbet (Cambridge: Cambridge University Press, 1991); *Hegel's Philosophy of Right*, trans. T.M. Knox (London: Oxford University Press, 1952) (first published 1942, not 1952 as most subsequent printings state). But Gans was not the author of these editions. The Wood-Nisbet edition critically compares the text of each of Gans's "Additions" with the student manuscript notes upon which each is based. The translator emphasizes the liberty that Gans took in paraphrasing the sources, *Elements of the Philosophy of Right*, xxxvi; it is remarkable, however, how little of the text is attributable to Gans. See *ibid.*, 13 (Gans added one word), 190 (one word), 218 (seven words), 305 (part of sentence), 346 (sentence), 355 (one word), 363 (one sentence).

4. Sibree included Gans's "Preface to the First Edition" in his translation of the philosophy of history. Hegel, *Lectures on the Philosophy of History*, trans. J. Sibree (London: Henry G. Bohn, 1857), xii-xxiii. Gans's Preface was included in the many English and American editions of Sibree's translation that appeared up till the early twentieth century, though later omitted it. *Cf. The Philosophy of History*, trans. J. Sibree (New York: Dover Publications, Inc., 1956).

   Although Gans's preface to the *Philosophy of Law* was not translated, Dyde's preface to his translation is essentially a paraphrase of Gans's own preface. See *Hegel's Philosophy of Right*, trans. S.W. Dyde (London: George Bell & Sons, 1896), ix-xiii.
5. David Johnston observes in the Preface to *The Roman Law of Trusts* (Oxford: Clarendon Press, 1988), vii, "If the law of legacies and trusts was the favourite law of the Roman jurists, it has some claim now to be considered the least favourite law of Romanists."
6. Waszek identifies the rise of anti-Semitism as a key factor in the decline of interest in Gans. Waszek, ed., *Eduard Gans (1797–1839)*, 12–13. But racist ideologues like Treitschke appeared after Gans had already been largely forgotten. Moreover, the rise of anti-Semitism hardly explains why Gans was forgotten by the many intellectual currents that were not dominated by it.
7. The character Marius assumes many autobiographical features. Like Hugo, he was the son of a Napoleonic general, an unenthusiastic law student, and a participant in the revolution of 1832.
8. Victor Hugo, *Les Miserables*, trans. Charles E. Wilbour, part 4, book 2, chapter 4. The term *étoile*, translated literally by Wilbour as "star," also means a crack in glass – i.e., something that distorts vision.
9. See S.S. Prawer, *Heine's Jewish Comedy: A Study of his Portraits of Jews and Judaism* (Oxford: Clarendon Press, 1983), 13.
10. Decline of the Hegelian establishment in Berlin in the 1830s is discussed by John Edward Toews, *Hegelianism: The Path Toward Dialectical Humanism, 1805–1841* (Cambridge: Cambridge University Press, 1982), 203–23. Between 1835 and 1840 only one Hegelian was promoted to full professor. Ibid., 221.
11. Thibaut's command of facts and theoretical sophistication were "characterized by a soundness of knowledge, clearness of expression, perspicuity of arrangement, and a subtlety of depth of thought that have seldom been equalled by any writer on the subject and cannot be surpassed." George Long, *Two Discourses delivered in the Middle Temple Hall* (London: Knight, 1847), 41, as quoted in Nathaniel Lindley, Translator's Preface, *An Introduction to the Study of Jurisprudence; being a Translation of the General Part of Thibaut's System des Pandekten Rechts*, trans. by Nathaniel Lindley (London: William Maxell, 1855). Lindley's translation of Thibaut, now utterly forgotten, commanded suf-

ficient interest in its day to lead to its publication in America (Philadelphia, 1855), and to two authorized reprintings (Madras, 1879 and 1890).

12. *A Political Treatise*, in *The Chief Works of Benedict de Spinoza*, 2 vols., trans. R.H.M. Elwes [actually this part translated by A.H. Gosset] (New York: Dover Publications, 1951), 1: 288.
13. Standard references often still give the year of his birth as March 22, 1798, e.g., *The New Encyclopedia Britannica: Micropaedia* (1985), 5: 112; *Brockhaus Enzyclopaedie* (Wiesbaden: F.A. Brockhaus, 1968), 6: 758–79; *Encyclopaedia Judaica* (Jerusalem: The Macmillan Company, 1971), 7: 311–12. But the most authoritative study of Gans gives his date of birth as March 23, 1797, see Hanns Günther Reissner, *Eduard Gans: Ein Leben im Vormärz*, Schriftenreihe Wissenschaftlicher Abhandlungen of the Leo Baeck Institut, vol. 14 (Tübingen: J.C.B. Mohr, 1965), 14.
14. Heine, born the same year as Gans, actually converted before Gans in 1825, yet he never forgave Gans for converting. The relation between Gans and Heine is the subject of sèveral probing discussions. In addition to Prawer, 1–43, who demonstrates convincingly that the evolution of Heine's attitudes towards Gans projected Heine's conflicted feelings about his own conversion, see the discussions in Norbert Waszek, Introduction to Édouard Gans, *Chroniques françaises: Un hégélien juif á Paris (1825, 1830, 1835)*, ed. Norbert Waszek and trans. Myriam Bienenstock, Bibliothèque franco-allemande (Paris: Les Éditions du Cerf, 1993), 27–42; Jean Pierre Lefebvre, *Der gute Trommler: Heines Beziehung zu Hegel*, Heine-Studien, ed. Joseph A. Kruse (Hamburg: Hoffman und Campe, 1986), 37, 66–72; Michel Espagne, *Federstriche; Die Konstruktion des Pantheismus in Heines Arbeitshandschriften*, Heine-Studien, ed. Joseph A. Kruse (Hamburg: Hoffman und Campe, 1991), 84–85.
15. Ludwig Philippson, *Allgemeine Zeitung des Judenthums*, vol. 3, no. 73 (June 18, 1839), 294–95, quoted and translated in Albert Hoschander Friedlander, "The Verein für Kultur und Wissenschaft der Juden: A Study in the History of Culture" (rabbinical dissertation, Hebrew Union College-Jewish Institute of Religion, Cincinnati campus, 1952), 48–49n.38.
16. *Spinoza and Other Heretics*, 2 vols. (Princeton University Press, 1988), 2: x. See also ibid., 1: x.
17. Lecture on the History of Law since 1789, from Felix Mendelssohn's student notes of the first lecture, quoted in Reissner, *Eduard Gans*, 126–27. Mendelssohn's notes survive and are located at the Leo Baeck Institute, New York. Reissner, *Eduard Gans*, 126n.1.
18. In his Preface to a collection of essays addressed to a broader, more popular audience than usual, Gans also remarked that the collection presented essays about men and relations that he had observed (*betrachten*). *Rückblicke auf Personen und Zustände* (Berlin: Verlag von Veit und Comp., 1836), v.
19. I believe this last sentence in the passage quoted in the text deliberately evokes the language from Spinoza's *Political Treatise* that I set forth apothegmatically at the head of this chapter. Gans's invocation of Spinoza in a lecture to a group of German students in the 1830s may suggest further that his lectures communicated on an esoteric level to a group of more cultured students. Gans lectured on Spinoza and specifically mentioned the *Political Treatise*; he referred again to this passage from it in his lectures on the philosophy of law in 1828–29. See Gans, "Naturrecht," in *Philosophische Schriften*, 56.
20. See Toews, *Hegelianism*, 108–09.
21. Reissner, *Eduard Gans*, 26, 33. Reissner may have misdated these presentations, which would seem more likely to have been made after Gans returned to Berlin.
22. Reissner, *Eduard Gans*, 44. He subsequently published a German language version of the dissertation as *Ueder* [*sic* for *Über*] *römisches Obligationsrecht, insbesondere über die Lehre von den Innominatcontracten und dem jus poenitendi: Drei civilistische Abhandlungen* (Heidelberg: Mohr und Winter, 1819).

23. For the history of the Historical School, see Franz Wieacker, *Privatrechtsgeschichte der Neuzeit unter besonderer Berücksichtigung der deutschen Entwicklung*, 2d ed. (Göttingen: Vandenhoeck & Ruprecht, 1967), 369, 371, 378; Gerhard Wesenberg and Gunter Wesener, *Neuere deutsche Privatrechtsgeschichte*, 4th improved ed. (Vienna and Cologne: Böhlau Verlag, 1985), 170, 171; Reissner, *Gans*, 41. For English language discussions, see Mathias Reimann, "Nineteenth Century German Legal Science," *Boston College Law Review* 31 (1990): 851–58; Susan Gaylord Gale, "A Very German Legal Science: Savigny and the Historical School," *Stanford Journal of International Law* 18 (1982): 123–46.
    Savigny's influence on American jurisprudence is discussed by Mathias Reimann, "The Historical School against Codification: Savigny, Carter, and the Defeat of the New York Civil Code," *The American Journal of Comparative Law* 37 (1989): 97–101.
24. See James Q. Whitman, *The Legacy of Roman Law in the German Romantic Era: Historical Vision and Legal Change* (Princeton: Princeton University Press, 1990), 79–80.
25. Whitman argues that the academic differences between Berlin and Heidelberg reflected differences in the regional legal cultures of Prussia and the "constitutional south." Whitman, *The Legacy of Roman Law in the German Romantic Era*, 98. Whitman modifies the traditional distinction between constitutional south and Prussian north by suggesting the presence of a third regional tradition in the north-central area that emphasized custom and tradition.
26. For a discussion of the intellectual context of the debate about codification, see Whitman, *The Legacy of Roman Law in the German Romantic Era*, 102–112.
27. For the best discussion of this critical period in Gans's intellectual biography, see Norbert Waszek's introduction to Édouard Gans, *Chroniques françaises: Un hégélien juif á Paris (1825, 1830, 1835)*, ed. Norbert Waszek and trans. Myriam Bienenstock, Bibliothèque franco-allemande (Paris: Les Éditions du Cerf, 1993), 17–19.
28. Holborn lists Berlin, Göttingen, and Leipzig as the only three non-Catholic universities at which there was little or no student activism. Hajo Holborn, *A History of Modern Germany 1648–1840* (New York: Alfred A. Knopf, 1964), 464.
29. See Reissner, *Eduard Gans*, 110.
30. See John E. Toews, "The Immanent Genesis and Transcendent Goal of Law: Savigny, Stahl, and the Ideology of the Christian German State," *The American Journal of Comparative Law* 37 (1989): 154.
31. Reissner, *Eduard Gans*, 48.
32. Toews, *Hegelianism*, 110.
33. Reissner, *Eduard Gans*, 49.
34. See generally Holborn, *A History of Modern Germany 1648–1840*, 465–71.
35. The Union had roots in an informal group of Berlin Jewish intellectuals that gathered as early as 1816. Gans and other founders of the Union participated in the earlier group. But topics in 1816 were cosmopolitan, historical, and literary; with few explicitly Jewish topics. Hillmar presented one talk on the Ancient History of the Jews; Moser presented one about Moses Mendelssohn and Evidence. Reissner, *Eduard Gans*, 33–34; Friedlander, "The Verein für Kultur und Wissenschaft der Juden," 30.
36. Reissner, *Eduard Gans*, 50. A list of the Union's members and their positions is appended. Ibid., 174–86. Its most famous member was the great poet Heinrich Heine, who joined in 1822. Ibid., 176.
37. Reissner, *Eduard Gans*, 50. Gans coined the term "science of Jews," see Friedlander, 31, came up with the official name for the Union, and helped draft its bylaws. Mendes-Flohr and Reinharz point out that the genitive ("of the Jews") was designedly equivocal – as Jews were both the scholars and subjects of scholarship. Mendes-Flohr and Reinharz, eds., *The Jew in the Modern World*, 189n.1.

38. Immanuel Wohlwill, "Über den Begriff einer Wissenschaft des Judentums," *Zeitschrift fuer die Wissenschaft des Judentums* 1 (1822): 1, quoted in Reissner, *Eduard Gans*, 64–65. See also the English translation in *Leo Baeck Institute Yearbook* 2 (1957): 194–204, and Mendes-Flohr and Reinharz eds., *The Jew in the Modern World*, 194–95.
    The bylaws of the Union that were adopted in August 1821 are translated by J. Hessing and P. Mendes-Flohr, in Mendes-Flohr and Reinharz, eds., *The Jew in the Modern World*, 188–89. The bylaws announced the need to reform the self-conception of the Jewish community by means of the activity of an intellectual elite. To that end, the bylaws called for the establishment of a scientific institute, archives, a journal, and a school.
39. Gans adopted Hegelian terminology (*aufzuheben*) and, perhaps to a lesser extent, the Hegelian view of the family's role in society. "Erste Rede vor dem 'Kulturverein'," Waszek ed., *Eduard Gans (1797–1839)*, 59.
40. Other scholars have read the first address as expressing a greater commitment to Hegelian philosophy. See, e.g., Toews, *Hegelianism*, 126.
41. *Halbjähriger Bericht im Verein für Cultur und Wissenschaft der Juden*, in Waszek, ed., *Eduard Gans (1797–1839)*, 62–75. Most of Gans's second address is translated by J. Hessing in Mendes-Flohr and Reinharz eds., *The Jew in the Modern World*, 190–93. Gans cites "one of the greatest religious thinkers and writers" as stating, "There is coming a time when no one in Europe will ask any longer who is Jewish and who is Christian." Waszek, ed., *Eduard Gans (1797–1839)*, 67; Mendes-Flohr and Reinharz eds., *The Jew in the Modern World*, 192. Waszek identified the text: Herder, *Ideen zur Philosophie der Geschichte der Menschkeit* [1791], in *Herders Sämmtliche Werke*, 33 vols., ed. Bernhard Suphan (Berlin: Wiedmannsche Buchhandlung, 1877–1913), 14 (1909): 284.
42. 1822 Address, trans. J. Hessing, in Mendes-Flohr and Reinharz, eds., *The Jew in the Modern World*, 191.
43. Ibid., 192. L. Sachs suggests that Gans's image provoked critical reactions from Jewish writers as late as 1860. See Samuel David Luzatto, "Learning based on Faith," trans. L. Sachs, in Mendes-Flohr and Reinharz, eds., *The Jew in the Modern World*, 230n.3.
44. Ibid., 193.
45. Édouard Gans, *Chroniques Françaises*, 20–22; Johann Braun, "Die 'Lex Gans' – ein Kapitel aus der Geschichte der Judenemanzipation in Preussen," *Zeitschrift der Savigny-Stiftung für Rechtsgeschichte*, Germanistische Abteilung 102 (1985): 62–98; Ismar Schorsch, "The Religious Parameters of Wissenschaft: Jewish Academics at Prussian Universities," *Yearbook Leo Baeck Institute* 25 (1980): 3–4.
46. Lionel E. Kochan remarks that Gans's acceptance of the grant was an act of acquiescence that irreparably undermined Gans' moral authority with the society, obliging him to withdraw." Immanuel Wolf, "On the Concept of a Science of Judaism," trans. Lionel E. Kochan, in Mendes-Flohr and Reinharz, eds., *The Jew in the Modern World*, 195n.2.
47. See the letter of Gans, Zunz, and Moser to Noah of January 1, 1822, in *Publications of the American Jewish Historical Society* 20 (1911): 147–48, quoted in Friedlander, "The Verein für Kultur und Wissenschaft der Juden," 51. The reference to Ganstown occurs in Heine's letter to Moser of May 23, 1823, quoted in S.S. Prawer, *Heine's Jewish Comedy*, 29, though Gans's contemporaneous writings suggest strongly that he had himself lost interest in the idea by mid–1823.
48. A total of six members of the Union converted. See Reissner, 174–85. Gans – unlike Heine – left no record of his personal response to his conversion. This apparently has led some to conclude that the conversion was "purely external and formal." Toews, *Hegelianism*, 130. Felix Eberty much later attributed to Gans the statement that the conversion recognized something "which I do not believe and which even the Minister knows perfectly well that I do not believe. . ." Felix Eberty, *Jugenderinnerungen eines alten Berliners* (Berlin: Verlag für Kulturpolitik, 1925), 313. But the authenticity of the statement is very doubtful; it is even questionable from the text whether Eberty meant

the quote to be understood as Gans's words or rather as words that articulated Gans's general attitude. Eberty would hardly have been a confidante of Gans. And his portrayal of the conversion as an empty gesture is consistent with his exaggerated treatment of Gans's Jewish features and his portrayal of the debate between Gans and Savigny as a racial conflict. Ibid., 311.

49. Reissner, *Eduard Gans*, 117. *Hegel: The Letters*, trans. by Clark Butler and Christiane Seiler with comm. by Clark Butler (Bloomington: Indiana University Press, 1984), 504.
50. Heine recalled that Gans spent evenings with Rahel Varnhagen, a converted Jew. Prawer, 24, 738.
51. His autobiographical notice is striking for what it does not say: it is completely silent as to his Jewish heritage and omits any mention of religious feelings or personal relationships altogether.
52. Reissner, *Eduard Gans*, 158. In mitigation, Reissner suggests that Gans's mental health may have been failing at the time. Gans's hostility to the full participation of Jews in the academy is deplorable, but little is known other than the fact that Gans signed the petition. His position may have reflected increasing irritation at what he perceived to be the growing intransigence and parochialism among Jewish thinkers.
53. Eduard Gans, *Über die Grundlage des Besitzes: Eine Duplik* (Berlin, Verlag von Veit und Comp., 1839), 2–3.
54. Letter from Gans to Athanase Jourdan of April 13, 1826, in "Eduard Gans' Briefe an Athanase Jourdan," ed. Norbert Waszek, *Hegel-Studien* 22 (1987): 39. Gans remarked in his next letter, June 25, that the course on the Law of Succession was more successful.
55. The course title varied slightly but was offered Winter 1827, Winter 1829, Winter 1830. Reissner, *Eduard Gans*, 125, 138, 142, 147.
56. He offered a course on Inheritance in Summer 1827, Summer 1828, Summer 1829, summer 1830, *Ibid.*, 125, 126, 129, 138, 147.
57. The course listings are identified for only some years in Reissner, *Eduard Gans*, 125, 126, 129, 138, 142, 157.
58. Hegel had previously lectured on Natural Law three times but gave the course over to Gans in 1825. See the editor's note in *Briefe von und an Hegel*, 4 vols., 3rd ed., ed. by Johannes Hoffmeister (Hamburg: Felix Meiner Verlag, 1969), 3: 472.
59. This episode is described by Clark Butler in *Hegel: The Letters*, 676. I treat it in the next section.
60. Gans was powerfully affected by French ideas and by his visits to Paris in 1825, 1830, and 1835. For Gans's relation to France, see Norbert Waszek, Introduction to Édouard Gans, *Chroniques françaises*, 76–100.
61. Waszek, ed., *Eduard Gans (1797–1839)*, 26.
62. Toews suggests that both liberal and conservative readers had interpreted Hegel's Philosophy of Law as a rationalization for the status quo of the reaction. *Hegelianism*, 96. But Gans's Preface (if it is autobiographically accurate) demonstrates that some readers interpreted the work as a progressive and historical treatment that implied a powerful criticism of the current political establishment.
63. Toews, *Hegelianism*, 121.
64. See letter of Gans (February 28, 1826), in "Eduard Gans' Briefe an Athanase Jourdan," 37.
65. Gans, Preface to Hegel's *Philosophy of Law*. See part 3.
66. See Waszek, "The Stagnation of the Consciousness of Freedom," 179.
67. *Beiträge zur Revision der preussischen Gesetzgebung* (Berlin: Duncker und Humblot, 1830–32). A total of six parts (of the first volume) appeared.
68. "Zur preussischen Verfassungsfrage," in *Beiträge zur Revision der preussischen Gesetzgebung* (1832), reprinted in Waszek, ed., *Eduard Gans (1797–1839)*, 148–49.
69. Ibid., 153–54.

70. The clearest exposition of his doctrine of the Opposition appeared posthumously. Letter to Dr. Dorow in Berlin, in *Denkschriften und Briefe zur Charakteristik der Welt und Litteratur* 5 (Berlin, 1841): 90–93, in Waszek, ed., *Eduard Gans (1797–1839)*, 155–56.
71. See Norbert Waszek, "Eduard Gans on Poverty: Between Hegel and Saint-Simon," *Owl of Minerva* 18 (1987): 167–78; idem, "Eduard Gans und die Armut: Von Hegel und Saint-Simon zu frühwerkschaftlichen Forderungen," *Hegel-Jahrbuch 1988*, ed. Heinz Kimmerle, Wolfgang Lefèvre, and Rudolf W. Meyer (Bochum: Germinal Verlag, 1988); idem, "La Réception du Saint-Simonisme dans l'école hégélienne: l'exemple d'Eduard Gans," *Archives de Philosophie* 52 (1989): 581–87. Hegel had, of course, addressed the problem of poverty, but Hegel had been concerned with poverty as an economic problem that prevented or retarded social integration rather than as a central problem of social justice. See Harry Brod, *Hegel's, Philosophy of Politics: Idealism, Identity, and Modernity* (Boulder: Westview Press, 1992), 107.
72. Reissner, *Eduard Gans*, 157. Though some writers have argued that Marx was influenced by these lectures, Reissner rightly emphasizes the weakness of the evidence. Ibid., 158.
73. Waszek, ed., *Eduard Gans (1797–1839)*, 39. Norbert Waszek, "Zwischen Hegel un Marx: Eine Würdigung Eduard Gans' anlässlich der 150. Wiederkehr seines Todestages," *Dialektik* 17 (1989): 170–74. The direct evidence consists chiefly of the facts that Marx enrolled in Gans's courses at Berlin and relied on Gans's posthumous edition of Hegel's *Philosophy of Law*. The internal evidence of influence based on similarities is more conjectural. E.g., ibid., 172.
74. "Autobiographische Notiz," in Waszek, ed., *Eduard Gans (1797–1839)*, 54–55.
75. There is a long tradition of describing Gans as a Right Hegelian, and the description has even motivated efforts to rehabilitate Right Hegelianism. See Toews, *Hegelianism*, 396n.8. This confusion still appears in the scholarship. For example, Brazill writes: "The Hegelians of the right affirmed the Christian faith and affirmed the existing institutions of society as the embodiment of the divine. Eduard Gans was the philosopher of law who based his views on the conservative interpretation of Hegel." William J. Brazill, *The Young Hegelians* (New Haven: Yale University Press, 1970), 50. He gives no reason for characterizing Gans as a conservative, however, and seems unfamiliar with Gans's writings or biography. Perhaps, he assumed Gans was a conservative because of his role in editing Hegel's works, for the posthumous editors did include a number of conservative Hegelians.
76. Toews most fully expounds the view of Gans in anticipating and encouraging the emergence of critical Hegelianism. *Hegelianism*, 228–29.
77. Reissner, *Eduard Gans*, 159. One wonders whether the intensity of Gans's intellectual activity did not reflect a certain awareness of his own mortality, for his father had died suddenly at the age of forty-seven. Ibid., 21.
78. Letter to his wife and children, August 17, 1826, in *Hegel: The Letters*, 506.
79. *Georg Wilhelm Friedrich Hegel's Werke*, 18 vols., complete edition by a society of the friends of the deceased, Ph. Marheineke, J. Schulze, Ed. Gans, Lp. v. Henning. H. Hotho, K. Michelet, F. Förster (Berlin: Verlag von Duncker und Humblot, 1832–45), vol. 8: *George Wilhelm Friedrich Hegel's Grundlinien der Philosophie des Rechts; oder Naturrecht und Staatswissenschaft im Grundrisse*, ed. Eduard Gans (1833). Gans provided a Preface and appended extensive "Additions" to Hegel's outline from the manuscript lecture notes of two students.

    Modern scholars typically complain about the lack of "scrupulous philological accuracy" of Gans's treatment of the student notes. Translator's Preface, G.W.F. Hegel, *Elements of the Philosophy of Right*, xxxvi. But Gans's edition surpassed the editorial standards of his day. Gans's selection of notes arguably helped make the *Philosophy of Law* one of Hegel's most accessible texts, and the one most frequently translated into English.

Gans's selection of Additions (but not his Preface) have been retained by most subsequent German editors and are included in the best English translations.

80. *Vorlesungen über die Philosophie der Geschichte*, ed. Eduard Gans (Berlin, 1837). Gans's careful treatment of the text of the lectures compares favorably with the "revision" of Gans's work by Karl Hegel and with the English translations by Sibree and Hartman. See Walter Kaufmann, *Hegel: A Reinterpretation* (Garden City: Doubleday & Company, Inc., 1966), 382–83.
81. In a letter to his wife and children on July 29, 1826, Hegel explained how he passed his time, "In the evening I have Gans or some other friend over. . ." *Hegel: The Letters*, 184.
82. Manfred Riedel, "Eduard Gans, discepolo di Hegel: Per l'interpretazione politica della filosofia del diritto," trans. Gianstefano Villa, *Rivista di filosofia* 68 (1977): 254–55; Editor's Introduction, Hegel, *Elements of the Philosophy of Right*, xxii.
83. Arnold Ruge, "Hegel's *Philosophy of Right* and the Politics of our Times," [trans. James A. Massey?], in Lawrence S. Stepelevich ed., *The Young Hegelians: An Anthology* (Cambridge: Cambridge University Press, 1983), 219.
84. Manfred Riedel relates Gans's more enthusiastic reception of current events in France to important differences from Hegel on philosophy of history and law. "Eduard Gans als Schüler Hegels: Zur politischen Auslegung der Rechtsphilosophie," *Rivista di Filosofia* 68 (1977): 242–47, 251–52.
85. Clark Butler recounts the story from various sources in *Hegel: The Letters*, 676.
86. The announcements of Hegel's fall courses for 1831–32 listed 1) philosophy of law and 2) the first part of the philosophy of history. Whatever the history of the announcements or reasons for the change, it is clear that Hegel's interest in teaching the philosophy of law predated any political pressure associated with his meeting with the Crown Prince in 1831. See *Dokumente und Materialien zur Biographie*, ed. Friedhelm Nicolin, in *Briefe von und an Hegel*, 4: 118, 124.
87. *Hegel: The Letters*, 676.
88. Various student manuscript notes survive of Gans's lectures on Natural Law. Some have been published. Gans, *Philosophische Schriften*, includes notes from the 1828–29 lectures; idem., *Naturrecht und Universalrechtsgeschichte*, includes notes from the 1832–33 lectures.
89. This structure is clear in the lectures of 1828–29 and 1832–33, and I derive it from the text of the lectures rather than the outline provided by the editors. The editorial outlines suggest a change in Gans's organization by placing "the good" as a subcategory of "happiness." Such a change suggests that Gans's later lectures moved away from Hegel's triadic formalism and might even suggest a more substantive departure from Hegel's treatment of morality. Compare the outline for 1828–29 in Gans, *Philosophische Schriften*, 37 and the outline for 1832–33 in Gans, *Naturrecht und Universalrechtsgeschichte*, 7. The former outline is inaccurate, however, for the material on The Good, which follows the rubric "Third part of Morals, On the Highest Good," plainly has equal status in the system with the preceding material on Happiness and is not a subpart of Happiness.

    My reading is not only consistent with Hegel's system, it is the only organization that comports with the enumeration and the text. Happiness, as the "Doctrine of Goals," is "the second part of Morals," Gans, *Philosophische Schriften*, 93, line 1, and the material on The Good is "the third part of morals," *not* of Happiness of Goals, which has no enumerated subparts. Ibid., 96.
90. For a comparative discussion of Gans's approach in the lectures in 1828–29 and 1832–33 that concludes that there are significant changes in Gans's treatment of poverty, which differs from Hegel's, see Norbert Waszek, "Eduard Gans on Poverty," 170, 172. See also Waszek, "La Réception du Saint-Simonisme dans l'école hégélienne: l'exemple d'Eduard Gans," 581–87.

91. Manfred Riedel correctly insists that the double title is not just a subtitle. *Between Tradition and Revolution: The Hegelian Transformation of Political Philosophy*, trans. Walter Wright (Cambridge: Cambridge University Press, 1984), 162–63.
92. Gans, *Naturrecht und Universalrechtsgeschichte*, 54.
93. H.B. Acton, Introduction, G.W.F. Hegel, *Natural Law: The Scientific Ways of Treating Natural Law, its Place in Moral Philosophy, and its Relation to the Positive Sciences of Law*, trans. T.M. Knox (N.p.: University of Pennsylvania Press, 1975), 16.
94. Gans, *Philosophische Schriften*, 56–60 (reading Wolff for Wolf), 68.
95. This also imparted a more historical content to Gans's treatment of law, and thus Riedel and Waszek are justified in describing Gans as propounding a "theory of the historicization of law." Waszek, Introduction to Édouard Gans, *Chroniques françaises*, 57; Riedel, "Einleitung," in Gans, *Naturrecht und Universalrechtsgeschichte*, 13.
96. See Hegel, *Elements of the Philosophy of Right*, 185–89, secs. 141–42.
97. Gans, *Philosophische Schriften*, 99. While the terminology *Recht der Sittlichkeit* does not appear in the transcript of the 1832–33 lectures, Gans there, too, insisted on a more direct connection between order based on custom (*Sittlichkeit*) and law proper than did Hegel, explaining, "Man has [legal] rights only insofar as he has duties, and duties only insofar as he has rights." Gans, *Naturrecht und Universalrechtsgeschichte*, 75.
98. Gans, *Philosophische Schriften*, 104.
99. Ibid., 104.
100. Hegel, *Elements of the Philosophy of Right*, 219, sec. 181.
101. Gans, *Philosophische Schriften*, 105. Gans ascribed a more positive role to the family in history, too. He saw modern German succession law as a positive historical achievement and also saw the Reformation as reinvigorating family relationships. See his lectures on Universal Legal History, *Naturrecht und Universalrechtsgeschichte*, 154.
102. See *Hegel: The Letters*, 505.
103. See Eduard Gans, "Die Stiftung der Jahrbücher für wissenschaftliche Kritik," in *Rückblicke auf Personen und Zustände*, 229, 231, 234–35. For the text of the bylaws, see the transcription of F. Hogemann, in Christoph Jamme, *Die "Jahrbücher für wissenschaftliche Kritik": Hegels Berliner Gegenakademie* (Frommann-Holzboog, 1994), 88–92.
104. Reissner, *Eduard Gans*, 118–20.
105. Gans's role in the Yearbooks and the influence of French political journalism is discussed by Norbert Waszek, "Eduard Gans, die 'Jahrbücher für wissenschaftliche Kritik' und die französische Publizistik der Zeit," in Christoph Jamme, ed., *Die "Jahrbücher für wissenschaftliche Kritik": Hegels Berliner Gegenakademie* (Frommmann-Holzboog, 1994), 93–118. Waszek lists Gans's reviews, ibid., 117–18. It is interesting to speculate about how much Gans's – and, indirectly, Hegel's – idea of a dissident academy was influenced by the experience of the Union for the Culture and Science of Jews.
106. *Briefe von und an Hegel*, 3: 32. The book's preface was dated March 23, 1823, and this letter to Hegel confirms that it was published the year before the publication date on its two title pages, Eduard Gans, *Das Erbrecht in weltgeschichtlicher Entwickelung: Eine Abhandlung der Universalrechtsgeschichte*, vol. 1; and *Das römische Erbrecht in seiner Stellung zu vor- und nach-römischen: Eine Abhandlung der Universalrechtsgeschichte*, vol. 1 (Berlin: Maurerschen Buchhandlung, 1824).
107. Undated letter to Savigny, quoted in Johann Braun, "Schwan und Gans: Zur Geschichte des Zerwürfnisses zwischen Friedrich Carl von Savigny und Eduard Gans," in *Juristenzeitung* 34 (December 14, 1979): 770. The fact that Gans refers in this letter to "our science" is an important reminder that the term "science" did not yet in 1819 necessarily imply Hegelian philosophy for Gans. With this letter Gans sent Savigny a copy of his book *Ueder* [*sic*] *römisches Obligationsrecht*. Since the Preface to the book is dated September 1819, he must have sent this letter to Savigny in late 1819 or early 1820.
108. *Das Erbrecht*, 1: xxxi.

109. The work appeared in four volumes: volume one (1824) treated oriental and Greek law; volume two (1825) treated Roman Law; volume three (1829) treated Canon Law and the reception of the Roman Law of inheritance in Italy, Spain, and Portugal; and volume four (1835) treated the law of inheritance in France, England, Scandinavia, and Scotland. Gans never completed the project. He announced further volumes five and six, which never appeared. Gans, *Das Erbrecht*, 4: xiv. Reissner suggests that psychological obstacles prevented Gans from completing the work; others suggest that he was engaged in too many simultaneous projects at the end of his life to finish any. See Waszek, "Eduard Gans on Poverty: Between Hegel and Saint-Simon," 169n.7. It is hard to avoid the inference, however, that the combination of inner personal convictions and outer political pressures that led Gans to define the project in the way that he did also made the completion of the project unthinkable.
110. Eduard Gans, *System des römischen Civilrechts im Grundrisse, nebst einer Abhandlung über Studium und System des römischen Rechts* (Berlin: bei Ferdinand Dümmler, 1827), 143.
111. *Zeitschrift fuer die Wissenschaft des Judenthums* 1 (1822–23): 419–71. The material appeared as chapter three in the book.
112. Gans's biographer suggests that the Hegelian influence stemmed from an intensive study of philosophy in 1820, but the source supporting the argument is dated May 4, 1823, *after* the completion of the first volume of the treatise and, indeed, roughly contemporaneous with the Preface. Reissner, *Eduard Gans*, 62n.5.
113. Some scholars believe that Gans came under the influence of both Thibaut and Hegel in Heidelberg. See Norbert Waszek, Introduction, Waszek, ed., *Eduard Gans (1797–1839)*, 15; Waszek, "Eduard Gans on Poverty: Between Hegel and Saint-Simon," 167n.1; Manfred Riedel, "Einleitung," in Gans, *Naturrecht und Universalrechtsgeschichte*, 12. Waszek has recently advanced the most sustained and persuasive effort to date Hegel's influence to Heidelberg. "Introduction," in Gans, *Chroniques françaises*, 43–44. But while he has proven that the early date is possible, there is still no conclusive evidence for placing the influence so early. Reissner, on the other hand, questioned placing the influence so early, see Reissner, *Eduard Gans*, 46.
114. Gans left Göttingen in August and enrolled September 1, 1818 at Heidelberg. Reissner, *Eduard Gans*, 44. Hegel was still in Heidelberg in early September but arrived at Berlin by early October. See *Brief von und an Hegel* 2: 197–203.
115. Gans, "Rede bei der Wideröffnung der Sitzungen des Vereins für Cultur und Wissenschaft der Juden," in Waszek, ed., *Eduard Gans (1797–1839)*, 59. Waszek points out the Hegelian influence on the passage, ibid., 22.
116. Eduard Gans, *Ueder* [*sic*] *römisches Obligationsrecht*, ix, 9. Gans's reference to the "universal perspective" and "progress of science" in the Preface *may* suggest exposure to Hegelian ideas, but the terms were also widespread. His use of the term "concept" to connote a vague collection of miscellaneous topics, ibid., 133, is strikingly un-Hegelian.
117. Eduard Gans, *Scholien zum Gaius* (Berlin: bei Ferdinand Dummler, 1821). Gans completed the manuscript in 1820, and the Preface is dated October 10, 1820, Berlin.
118. See Editor's Introduction, Hegel, *Elements of the Philosophy of Right*, xxxiv.
119. Gans, Preface, in Hegel, *Grundlinien der Philosophie des Rechts*, ed. Eduard Gans, in *Werke*, 8: 17. If the observation is taken as biographically accurate, it further confirms that Gans was not significantly influenced by Hegel in Heidelberg.
120. Gans, "A Society to Further Jewish Integration," 193. The text in brackets is interpolated by the translator, J. Hessing.
121. In this respect, I disagree with Friedlander's explanation of Gans's conversion: "Gans was a Hegelian; he implicitly believed all that Hegel signified in the field of law. But how could he accept Hegel on this point and not on the other aspects of his life? Through Hegel, he had come to believe that Christianity represented the most advanced development of the

history of thought. . ." Friedlander, "The Verein für Kultur und Wissenschaft der Juden," 43. But it was not doctrinal, Lutheran Christianity that represented this apex for Hegel but rather the scientific expression (i.e., in philosophy) of all historical developments (including Jewish culture). And reconciling this philosophical vision with the reality of state religion necessitated an elastic, equivocating treatment of Christian religion.

122. Gans would probably have had no inkling that the onset of the reaction in 1819 had affected Hegel sufficiently to have caused him to delay and rework *The Philosophy of Law*.
123. "Autobiographische Notiz," in Waszek, ed., *Eduard Gans (1797–1839)*, 53–55. The notice was published in 1840, but from internal evidence Waszek dates it to early 1835. Ibid.,42
124. Lectures on Natural Law and Universal History of Law, 1823–33, transcribed by Immanuel Hegel, in Gans, *Naturrecht und Universalrechtsgeschichte*, 37.
125. Savigny had written, "Justinian's plan embraced the two principal objects of abridging, in separate works, the Jurists, and the Constitutions. The first, or the Pandects, was very properly intended to contain the fundamental principles of the law; and it was the only work, since the Twelve Tables, which, in itself complete, and without reference to another, might be considered as a centre point, from which the whole law emanated. In this respect, it may be called a Code of Laws, and the first full comprehensive Code since the Twelve Tables. . ." Carl von Savigny, *The History of the Roman Law during the Middle Ages*, trans. E. Cathcart (Edinburgh: Adam Black, 1829), 15.
126. Whitman, *The Legacy of Roman Law in the German Romantic Era*, 110–11.
127. Discussions of Savigny almost always emphasize that he did not oppose all codes. But in fact, when Savigny served as member of the State Council and as judge on the Berlin Court of Appeal and Cassation for the Rhine Provinces in the 1820s, he persistently limited the extension of the Prussian Code and worked to abolish the indigenous versions of the Napoleonic Code in the provinces. See Toews, "The Immanent Genesis and Transcendent Goal of Law," 154.
128. *System des römischen Civilrechts*, 155–57.
129. Ibid., 157.
130. Ibid., 142–43.
131. *Rückblicke auf Personen und Zustände*, 250.
132. *System des römischen Civilrechts*, 152–53.
133. Ibid., 175.
134. Gans was assigned the course on the Digest for the winter term 1827, and he wrote Athanase Jourdan on June 25, 1826 that he would give "a course of exegesis and I [will] explain select laws from the Digest." "Eduard Gans' Briefe an Athanase Jourdan," 42.
135. *System des römischen Civilrechts*, nn. 7, 8, 12, 13, 18, 22, 40, 62, 68, 89, 90, 91, 92, 93, 98, 110, 132, 143, 151, 153, 156, 159, 169, 171, 178, 180, 181, 196, 197, 200.
136. Ibid., nn. 194, 195.
137. Ibid., nn. 61, 82, 101, 137, 139. 147, 162, 188, 189, 190.
138. Ibid., n. 175.
139. Ibid., n. 173.
140. Ibid., n. 137.
141. Gans's major life work begins with a long quotation from Thibaut. See Eduard Gans, *Das Erbrecht in weltgeschichtlicher Entwickelung*, 1: iv.
142. Anton Friedrich Justus Thibaut, *System des Pandekten-Rechts*, 2 vols. (Jena: Mauke, 1803); idem, 2nd improved and expanded ed., 3 vols. (Jena: Mauke, 1805–06); idem, 3rd ed., 3 vols. [in 1] (Jena: Mauke, 1809); idem, 4th ed., 3 vols. (Jena: Mauke, 1814); idem, 5th ed., 3 vols. (Jena: Mauke, 1818); idem, 6th ed., 3 vols. [in 2] (Jena: Friedrich Mauke, 1823); idem, 7th ed., 2 vols. [in 1] (Jena: Friedrich Mauke, 1828); idem, 8th ed., 2 vols. (Jena: Friedrich Mauke, 1834). Publication dates given in the text above are taken from

the dates of prefaces reprinted in the sixth edition. For example the preface to the sixth edition was dated May 1822, and it most likely appeared before the fall of 1822 despite the fact that the title page places its publication in 1823.

My research is based on the sixth edition, and I have not compared variant texts. Though the prefaces to previous editions do not suggest that there were drastic changes, there are striking differences between the sixth edition and the posthumously edited ninth edition. Idem, 9th ed., 2 vols., posthumously edited by Alexander August v. Buchholtz (Jena: Friedrich Mauke, 1846). For an English translation of the latter, the only legal work of Thibaut's translated into English, see idem, *An Introduction to the Study of Jurisprudence; Being a Translation of the General Part of Thibaut's System des Pandekten Rechts.*

143. In the eighth edition he explained his division of the book into a general part and particular part, and his further division of the particular part into the law of status, obligations, and real property and succession on pedagogical rather than logical grounds: "Whoever has had to teach beginners any developed historical science must have found himself compelled to abandon the plan of procedure dictated by strict logical principles, and so to arrange his matter that that which is first treated may render what follows as intelligible as possible. From considerations such as these, and no others, the author has be induced to divide the present work into four books..." Thibaut, *An Introduction to the Study of Jurisprudence*, 4 (from the eighth edition according to the accompanying translator's note).
144. Institutes 1.13–1.26, *Justinian's Institutes* trans. Peter Birks and Grant McLeod (Ithaca: Cornell University Press, 1987), 47–55. This treatment of guardianship relationships followed Gaius, Institutes 1.142–1.199. See *The Institutes of Gaius*, trans. W.M. Gordon and O.F. Robinson (Ithaca: Cornell University Press, 1988), 97–123.
145. See Hegel, *Elements of the Philosophy of Right*, 214–18, secs. 178–180.
146. "A legal system must present the content of laws in a systematic unity." Thibaut, *System des Pandekten-Rechts*, 7.
147. Thibaut, *System des Pandekten-Rechts*, 3–5.
148. Gans, *System of Roman Civil Law*, secs. 24 and 25.
149. Thibaut, *System des Pandekten-Rechts*, 26–27, sec. 33.
150. Ibid., 23–24, sec. 29.
151. Gans, *System of Roman Civil Law*, sec. 39.
152. Gans, *System of Roman Civil Law*, secs. 39–42. Thibaut divides laws into universal (subdivided into common and particular) and special. Thibaut, *System des Pandekten-Rechts*, 23–24, sec. 29.
153. Hegel had observed (incorrectly) that testamentary disposition required civil society and legislation. *Elements of the Philosophy of Right*, 111, sec. 80.
154. *System des römischen Civilrechts*, 174–75.
155. Ibid., 157.
156. In the Treatise, Gans praised Hegel's classification of contracts. *System des römischen Civilrechts*, 229–30, 232. His own System adopted the classification in presenting the material in secs. 197–258.
157. Ibid., 225. Gans's deviation from Hegel in retaining a separate place for torts in the scheme was the only occasion I am aware of where Gans expressly addressed (and justified) his deviation from Hegel.
158. Gans, *Naturrecht und Universalrechtsgeschichte*, 53. Compare his treatment of Hegel's system in lectures from 1828–29 as establishing the basis for the third part of the course coverage – practical law as the unity of philosophy and history. Gans, *Philosophischen Schriften*, 70.
159. For example, Gans categorized methods for acquiring property as 1) immediate acquisition, 2) acquisition mediated by a thing, and 3) acquisition mediated by another person. *System of Roman Civil Law*, sec. 116. He classified the laws of marriage under 1) cele-

bration of marriage, 2) laws regulating the marital relationship, and 3) laws regulating its dissolution. Ibid., secs. 301–19. Gans organized the treatment of the law of guardianship: 1) appointment, 2) legal relations, and 3) termination.

160. Goethe, *Faust*, 682f. The German has an explicit legal meaning and can be translated as: "That which has passed to you by inheritance from your ancestors, Acquire that you may possess it." The phrase thus refers to the legal need to enter an inheritance prior to possessing an estate, but the German verb (*erwerben*) for acquiring or obtaining property also connotes effort and merit on the part of the recipient. Thus the passage might be better translated as: "*Earn* what you have inherited from your fathers in order to possess it."
161. S.S. Prawer discusses the influence of Gans on this passage in *Heine's Jewish Comedy*, 42.
162. David Johnston, *The Roman Law of Trusts*, 2–5.
163. Johnston (following Gaius) lists three major differences: 1) the restrictions on persons who could take legacies did not apply to trusts, which could be left to anyone; 2) unlike legacies (which required a valid will), trusts could transfer property where the decedent died intestate; and 3) while legacies were only binding on the heir, trusts could impose a personal obligation on any beneficiary. *The Roman Law of Trusts*, 6.
164. "The flexibility of the substantive law of trusts is reflected in its procedural versatility. This versatility rested on two bases: first, the structure of the rights set up by trusts; second, the procedural system by which they could be enforced." Johnston, *The Roman Law of Trusts*, 254.
165. In 1820 Gans had organized the first of four sections on succession (the law of inheritance of freedmen) thus: 1) testamentary succession, 2) intestate succession, 3) bonorum possessio, and 4) legacy and testamentary trust. *Scholien zum Gaius* (Berlin: Ferdinand Dummler, 1821), 278.
166. Thibaut, *System des Pandekten-Rechts*, 2: 318–21, secs. 907–09.
167. Gans, Lectures from 1832–33, *Naturrecht und Universalrechtsgeschichte*, 80–81.
168. This was clear not just from his historical treatment in lectures on Natural Law but also from the *System of Roman Civil Law* itself, for his treatment of intestate succession comprised a survey of the historical recognition of new categories of heirs under Roman Law. *System of Roman Civil Law*, secs. 411–418.
169. Gans, *System of Roman Civil Law*, n.173, cites Cicero, and D. 50.17.7 (stating the principle prohibiting partial testacy), 29.2.19 (soldier's will), 29.1.37 (soldier's will), 29.2.39 (entrance into an inheritance accepted under a will), and 5.2.15.2 (son's action against two heirs succeeded against one). The clearest authority Gans found that Roman Law allowed partial intestacy was in his citation to the discussion of an action to divide an inheritance won by a son against one of two heirs. But the partial intestacy resulted from judgments issued by two different judges and might be limited to the unusual case where inconsistent *judgments* determined rights in an estate.
170. Friedrich Karl von Savigny, *Das Recht des Besitzes* (1803). A later edition of the work (containing Savigny's response to Gans's criticism) is translated as *Von Savigny's Treatise on Possession: Or, the Jus Possessionis of the Civil Law*, trans. Erskine Perry (Westport, Connecticut: Hyperion Press, 1979), 5, 31–32.
171. Reissner discusses Gans's last work, *Über die Grundlage des Besitzes: Eine Duplik* (1839), in the context of Gans's mental decline and likens its argument to Quixote's struggle against windmills. Reissner, *Eduard Gans*, 159.
172. "Autobiographische Notiz," in Waszek, ed., *Eduard Gans (1797–1839)*, 53, 54.
173. See letters of Gans (April 13, 1826 and June 25, 1826), in "Eduard Gans' Briefe an Athanase Jourdan," 39, 42.
174. For expressions of Gans's admiration, see Gans, *System des römischen Civilrechts*, 165, 174, 202. The fainthearted character of Gans's praise for Savigny is apparent when we

recall that Savigny's system was widely regarded both as its author's magnum opus and as one of the major legal works of the age; moreover, Gans immediately followed his praise in each instance by critical remarks about Savigny or the Historical School.

175. Ibid., 205.
176. Gans, *Über die Grundlage des Besitzes*, 10.
177. Ibid., 14.
178. Gans alluded critically to Savigny's theory of possession in 1828–29. Gans, *Philosophische Schriften*, 76. He criticized Savigny by name in 1832–33. Gans, *Naturrecht und Universalrechtsgeschichte*, 58.
179. The polemical content of his lectures may be fairly inferred from the prolonged criticism of the Historical School that Gans published in the corresponding part of Treatise. See *System des römischen Civilrechts*, 159–67.
180. Gans makes the polemical points that are implied by the System still more explicitly in the accompanying Treatise. Ibid., 181–82. His attack on the Historical School's preference for custom occurs immediately after his attack of that school's rejection of the Code: "It is remarkable that in recent times when customary law has lost almost all significance and when legislation is quick to provide an answer in order to prevent recourse to customary law – in a time marked so strongly by the power of the universal over the individual that the scope of self-legislation can hardly be accepted – there is so much talk of the excellence of customary law and the perniciousness of legislation." Ibid., 183.
181. Some of the rules determining bonorum possessio may have been promulgated by edict and others may have resulted from *ad hoc* decisionmaking. For a full discussion, see Alan Watson, *The Law of Succession in the Later Roman Republic* (Oxford: Clarendon Press, 1971), 71–84.
182. See Johnston, *The Roman Law of Trusts*, 222–55, 272, 274.
183. D. 30.1. See Johnston, *The Roman Law of Trusts*, 250–51,
184. See Glossary, *The Digest of Justinian*, 4 vols., ed. Theodor Mommsen and Paul Krueger, trans. Alan Watson (Philadelphia: University of Pennsylvania Press, 1985), 1: xvii.
185. William Blackstone, *Commentaries on the Laws of England, in Four Books*, 2: 10.
186. Christian wrote:

> I cannot agree with the learned Commentator, that the permanent right of property vested in the ancestor himself (that is, for his life), is not a natural, but merely a civil right.
>
> I have endeavoured to shew. . .that the notion of property is universal, and is suggested to the mind of man by reason and nature, prior to all positive institutions and civilized refinements. . . .I am obliged also to differ from the learned Judge, and all writers upon general law, who maintain, that children have no better claim by nature to succeed to the property of their deceased parents than strangers; and that the preference given to them, originates solely in political establishments.

Blackstone, *Commentaries on the Laws of England*, from the last London edition, ed. Edward Christian (Boston: T.B. Wait and Sons, 1818), 2: 11n.3.

187. Several different layers of commentary are apparent, for example, in *Commentaries on the Laws of England, in Four Books*, 19th ed., ed. J.E. Hovenden (London: S. Sweet and A. Maxwell, 1836), 2: 10–11nn.20–22. The editor replaced an earlier annotation from Christian that argued for a natural right of succession and in its place inserted authority from Locke that possessions revert to the community at death and are reallocated through laws of succession that express social convention rather than the individual's absolute rights.
188. Thus Christian related the natural right to property to the criminal sanctions for theft. *Commentaries on the Laws of England*, 4: 9n.8.

189. In *Goethe*, trans. and ed. David Luke (Baltimore: Penguin Books, 1964), 24–25.
190. Braun recounts details of the relation between Gans and Savigny that help explain Gans's personal bitterness and disappointment, see Braun, "Schwan und Gans," 773–75.
191. See Whitman, *The Legacy of Roman Law in the German Romantic Era*, 182–83.
192. Savigny, *Von Savigny's Treatise on Possession*, 409–417.
193. Whitman, *The Legacy of Roman Law in the German Romantic Era*, 183.
194. See Leonard Krieger, *The German Idea of Freedom: History of a Political Tradition* (Chicago: The University of Chicago Press, 1957).
195. *The Autobiography of Johann Wolfgang von Goethe*, trans. John Oxenford, 2 vols. (Chicago: The University of Chicago Press, 1974), 2: 149–50.
196. See his treatise, *System des römischen Civilrechts*, 225–26.
197. Gans, ed., *Beiträge zur Revision der preussischen Gesetzgebung*, pt. 1.
198. Eduard Gans, *System des römischen Civilrechts im Grundrisse, nebst einer Abhandlung über Studium und System des römischen Rechts* (Berlin: bei Ferdinand Dümmler, 1827).
199. See the letter from Gans to Athanase Jourdan (June 25, 1826), in "Eduard Gans' Briefe an Athanase Jourdan," ed. Norbert Waszek, *Hegel-Studien* 22 (1987): 42.
200. Reissner, *Eduard Gans*, 125, 126, 129, 138.
201. The treatise was composed after Gans had completed the system of Roman Law, though the preface to the first part, in referring to the treatise, obviously was written last.
202. See Gans, "Studium und System des römischen Rechts (1827)," in *Naturrecht und Universalrechtsgeschichte*, 191–236. The editor treats the treatise merely as part of Gans's polemic against the Historical School. Its title is slightly shortened; the book's title page was . . .*nebst Einer Abhandlung Über Studium und System des römischen Rechts* and the separate title page for the second part was *Über Studium und System des römischen Rechts*. This recent reprinting incorporates into its text those corrections identified on the original list of printer's errors.
203. E.g., *The Digest of Justinian*, 4 vols., Latin text ed. Theodor Mommsen with Paul Krueger, trans. Alan Watson (Philadelphia: University of Pennsylvania Press, 1985); *Justinian's Institutes*, trans. Peter Birks and Grant McLeod, with the Latin text of Paul Krueger (Ithaca: Cornell University Press, 1987); *The Institutes of Gaius*, trans. W.M. Gordon and O.F. Robinson, with the Latin text of Seckel and Kuebler (Ithaca: Cornell University Press, 1988).
204. Given the fidelity of the Latin and the sorts of errors that appeared repeatedly, it seems to be a fair inference that Gans provided the printer with a printed copy of the Latin material but indicated the citations with manuscript notes that were more easily misread. It is obvious that he did not proof read the notes with care, as only two printer's errors were listed at the end of the book, and both appeared in the second part of the book.
205. Though Gans cursorily proofread the page proofs so as to insert a list of Printer's Errors as the last, unnumbered page, the errata included only two spelling mistakes, and both occurred in the text of the *Treatise*. The inference that he did not proofread or copy edit the annotations to the system proper is consistent with my assumption that he composed the work rapidly during the summer of 1826.
206. *Gegenstand* and *Object* mean the same thing and are both rendered as "object." See sections 285–87. *Vermögens* and *Eigentum* are probably best both translated as "property," but to preserve Gans's distinction, the former is translated as "economic" (in compounds) or "assets."
207. "'Manners are stronger than laws.' . . . . Manners seem to say, *You are you, and I am I*." Ralph Waldo Emerson, *Letters and Social Aims* (Boston: James R. Osgood and Company, 1876), 73.
208. Waszek illustrates the importance of private law for understanding Gans's theory of the state when he points out that Gans considered the Prussian state a "state of guardianship [vormundschaftlicher Staat]." Norbert Waszek, "The Stagnation of the Consciousness

of Freedom: A Challenge to Hegelianism," in Henk Oosterling and Frans de Jong, ed., *Denken Unterwegs: Philosophie im Kräftefeld sozialen und politischen Engagements* (Amsterdam, Verlag B.R. Grüner, 1990), 180. Gans significantly adopted as his paradigm for the Prussian state the form of legal guardianship that applied to minors and that was transitional and temporary.

209. *Aufhebung*. Hegel's use of this term connoted simultaneous preservation, and it is usually rendered in English translations of Hegel's writing as "sublation." Here Gans seems to employ the term (like Schelling and other contemporaries) to mean cancellation proper.
210. Hegel, Preface, *Grundlinien der Philosophie des Rechts, Werke* 8: 17.
211. "Abandon all hope, you who enter here." Dante, *Divina commedia*, Inferno, iii.1.
212. *Gegensatz*.
213. *Geist* (spirit or mind). Gans does not mean to employ the term in its technical Hegelian sense here.
214. *sofort ein die Natur eines kernigen Niederschlags gewannen* continues the allusion to chemical condensation made earlier in the paragraph.
215. Hegel had lectured on the philosophy of law, using his *Encyclopedia of the Philosophical Sciences in Outline* (Heidelberg, 1817) as text in Heidelberg, 1817–18, and Berlin, 1818–19 and 1819–20. Gans mentions only those lectures for which the *Philosophy of Law* was the textbook. See the course announcements in Friedhelm Nicolin, *Dokumente und Materialien zur Biographie*, in *Briefe von und an Hegel*, 4 vols., new ed. (Hamburg: Felix Meiner Verlag, 1977): 4 (1): 111–25. Hegel announced the course in 1830–31 but did not offer it. Hegel's last course on the philosophy of law was to meet five days weekly at noon, and classes were scheduled to start October 24, but the commencement of the semester was postponed till November 7 because of the cholera epidemic. See ibid., 330–32. Classes apparently did not actually start till November 10, and Hegel lectured no more than three times before succumbing to cholera during the first weekend of the semester. He died November 14, 1831.
216. Sources that I consulted repeatedly in the translation and in compiling this Glossary include: Adolf Berger, *Encyclopedic Dictionary of Roman Law*, Transactions of the American Philosophical Society, n.s. vol. 43, part 2 (1953); Lewis and Short, *A New Latin Dictionary: Founded on the Translation of Freund's Latin-German Lexicon*, ed. E.A. Andrews, revised, enlarged, and rewritten by Charlton T. Lewis and Charles Short (New York: American Book Company, 1907); Alan Watson's glossary in *The Digest of Justinian*, 4 vols., ed. Theodor Mommsen and Paul Krueger, trans. Alan Watson (Philadelphia: University of Pennsylvania Press, 1985), 1: xv-xvii; *Black's Law Dictionary*, 5th ed. (St. Paul: West Publishing Co., 1979); William Blackstone, *Commentaries on the Laws of England; in Four Books*, 2 vols., ed. Thomas Cooley, 3d ed. (Chicago: Callaghan and Company, 1884); Alfred Romain *Wörterbuch der Rechts- und Wirtschaftssprache*, 2 vols., 2d ed. (Munich: C.H. Beck'sche Verlagsbuchhandlung, 1985); Clara-Erika Dietl et al., *Wörterbuch für Recht, Wirtschaft und Politik mit Kommentaren in deutscher und englisher Sprache*, 2 vols. (Munich: C.H. Beck'sche Verlagsbuchhandlung, 1983).
217. Karl Hegel's shorter and less important preface is still printed, perhaps because he was Hegel's son. Cf. "Charles Hegel's Preface," in Hegel, *The Philosophy of History*, trans. J. Sibree (New York: Dover Publications, Inc., 1956).
218. Hegel, *Philosophy of History*, trans. J. Sibree (London: Henry G. Bohn, 1857), xii-xxiii. A contemporaneous American edition also appeared, with spelling and punctuation altered. None of the alterations are significant, and they were presumably made by the American editors. The American edition dropped the footnote that cites the Bohn's edition of Schlegel for obvious reasons.
219. I have retained the mistaken spelling of "Grieshein" in the penultimate paragraph. It was corrected (to "Griesheim") in later editions.

BIBLIOGRAPHY

Works by Gans

Books and Monographs

Gans, Édouard. *Chroniques françaises: un hégélien juif à Paris (1825, 1830, 1835)*. Translated by Myriam Bienenstock. Edited with an Introduction by Norbert Waszek. Paris: Les Éditions de Cerf, 1993.

——. *Histoire du droit de succession en France, au Moyen Age*. Translated by L. De Loménie. Paris: Moquet et Challamel, 1845. [Partial translation of *Das Erbrecht*.]

Gans, Eduard. *Das Erbrecht in weltgeschichtlicher Entwickelung: Eine Abhandlung der Universalrechtsgeschichte*. 4 vols. 1824–35.

Most bibliographic citations to Gans's major life work fail to indicate that he switched publishers. Vol. 1: *Das römische Erbrecht in seiner Stellung zu vor- und nachrömischem: Eine Abhandlung der Universalrechtsgeschichte* (vol. 1). Berlin: Maurerschen Buchhandlung, 1824. Vol. 2: *Das römische Erbrecht in seiner Stellung zu vor- und nachrömischem: Eine Abhandlung der Universalrechtsgeschichte* (vol. 2). Berlin: Maurerschen Buchhandlung, 1825. Vol. 3: *Das Erbrecht des Mittelalters*. Stuttgart und Tübingen: J.G. Cotta'schen Buchhandlung, 1829. Vol. 4: *Das Erbrecht des Mittelalters* (second part). Stuttgart und Tübingen: J.G. Cotta'schen Buchhandlung, 1835. Reprinted 1962.

——. *Rückblicke auf Personen und Zustände*. Berlin: Verlag von Veit und Comp., 1836.

——. *Rückblicke auf Personen und Zustände*. New edition. Edited with an Introduction by Norbert Waszek. Spekulation und Erfahrung, division 1, vol. 4. Frommann-Holzboog, 1994.

——. *Scholien zum Gaius*. Berlin: bei Ferdinand Dümmler, 1821.

——. *System des römischen Civilrechts im Grundrisse, nebst einer Abhandlung über Studium und System des römischen Rechts*. Berlin: bei Ferdinand Dümmler, 1827.

——. *Über die Grundlage des Besitzes: Eine Duplik*. Berlin: Verlag von Veit und Comp., 1839.

——. *Ueder* [*sic* for *Über*]*römisches Obligationsrecht, insbesondere über die Lehre von den Innominatcontracten und dem* jus poenitendi: *Drei civilistische Abhandlungen*. Heidelberg: bei Mohr und Winter, 1819.

Three bibliographies give what appears to be a variant title of this work, *Über römisches Obligationsrecht, insbesondere über die fabelhafte Lehre von den Innominatcontracten und dem* jus poenitendi (Heidelberg, 1819). See Horst Schröder, Bibliographie in Gans, *Philosophische Schriften*, 389; Reissner, *Eduard Gans*, 191; Manfred Riedel, Bibliographie in Gans, *Naturrecht und Universalrechtsgeschichte*, 253.

——. *Urtheil eines Unparteiischen über das Benehmen der Juristenfacultät zu Berlin in der Habilitationsangelegenheit des Dr. Karl Witte*. Berlin and Frankfurt an der Oder, 1817.

——. *Vermischte Schriften, juristischen, historischen, staatswissenschaftlichen und ästhetischen Inhalts*. 2 Vols. Berlin: Duncker und Humblot, 1834.
——. *Vorlesungen über die Geschichte der letzten fünfzig Jahre*. Historisches Taschenbuch von Friedrich Raumer. Vol. 4 (Leipzig, 1833): 283–326. Vol. 5 (Leipzig, 1834): 409–53.

Articles, reviews, and component pieces

——. "Autobiographische Notiz." In *Hallische Jahrbuch für deutsche Wissenschaft und Kunst*. Vol 3 (1840): 902–03. Reprinted in Waszek, Norbert, ed. *Eduard Gans (1797–1839): Hegelianer-Jude-Europäer: Texte und Dokumente*. Hegeliana: Studien und Quellen zu Hegel und zum Hegelianismus, vol. 1. Series edited by Helmut Schneider. Frankfurt am Main: Peter Lang, 1991. Pp. 53–55.
——. "Dritter Bericht im Verein für Cultur und Wissenschaft der Juden." Hamburg: Otto, 1823. Reprinted in Waszek, Norbert, ed. *Eduard Gans (1797–1839): Hegelianer-Jude-Europäer: Texte und Dokumente*. Hegeliana: Studien und Quellen zu Hegel und zum Hegelianismus, vol. 1. Series edited by Helmut Schneider. Frankfurt am Main: Peter Lang, 1991. Pp. 55–62.
——. "Gesetzgebung über Juden in Rom, nach den Quellen des römischen Rechts." *Zeitschrift für die Wissenschaft des Judentums* 1 & 2 (1822). Republished as "Die Gesetzgebung über die Juden in Rom und die kirchlichen Würden derselben im Römischen Reich." *Vermischte Schriften, juristischen, historischen, staatswissenschaftlichen und ästhetischen Inhalts*, vol. 1.
——. "Die Grundzüge des mosaisch-talmudischen Erbrechts." *Zeitschrift für die Wissenschaft des Judentums* 1 (1822–23). Pp. 419–71. Republished in *Das Erbrecht in weltgeschichtlicher Entwickelung*, vol. 1, chap. 3, "Mosaisch-Talmudisches Erbrecht." Pp. 124–77.
——. "Halbjährlicher Bericht im Verein für Cultur und Wissenschaft der Juden." Hamburg: Hahn, 1822. Reprinted in Rubaschoff, S. ed. *Der jüdische Wille* (1919). Vol. 2. Pp. 109–15. Reprinted in Waszek, Norbert, ed. *Eduard Gans (1797–1839): Hegelianer-Jude-Europäer: Texte und Dokumente*. Hegeliana: Studien und Quellen zu Hegel und zum Hegelianismus, vol. 1. Series edited by Helmut Schneider. Frankfurt am Main: Peter Lang, 1991. Pp. 62–75.
——. "Nekrolog." [Obituary of Hegel.] *Allgemeine preussische Staatszeitung*. No. 333 (December 1, 1831): 1751–52. Reprinted in Waszek, Norbert, ed. *Eduard Gans (1797–1839): Hegelianer-Jude-Europäer: Texte und Dokumente*. Hegeliana: Studien und Quellen zu Hegel und zum Hegelianismus, vol. 1. Series edited by Helmut Schneider. Frankfurt am Main: Peter Lang, 1991. Pp. 102–06.
——. "Nachwort." *Zeitschrift für die Wissenschaft des Judentums* 3 (1823).
——. "Preface to the First Edition." Translated by J. Sibree. In Hegel, Georg. *Philosophy of History*. Translated by J. Sibree. London: Henry G. Bohn, 1857. Pp. xii-xxiii.
——. "Rede bei der Wiedereröffnung der Sitzungen des Vereins für Cultur und Wissenschaft der Juden," delivered in Berlin October 28, 1821. Hamburg, 1822. Pp. 5–16. Reprinted in Waszek, Norbert, ed. *Eduard Gans (1797–1839): Hegelianer-Jude-Europäer: Texte und Dokumente*. Hegeliana: Studien und Quellen zu Hegel und zum Hegelianismus, vol. 1. Series edited by Helmut Schneider. Frankfurt am Main: Peter Lang, 1991. Pp. 55–62.
——. Review of *Briefe aus Paris und Frankreich im Jahre 1830*, by Friedrich von Raumer, *Jahrbuch für wissenschaftliche Kritik*, 1831, pp. 339–52.
——. Review of *Des Abul-hassan Achmed Ben-Mohammed Koduri von Bagdad Moslemitisches Eherecht nach Hanifitischen Grundsätzen*, edited by Georg Helmsdörfer, *Jahrbuch für wissenschaftliche Kritik*, 1833, pp. 23–24.
——. Review of *Die Juden im preussischen Staate*, by C.F. Koch, *Jahrbuch für wissenschaftliche Kritik*, 1833, pp. 143–44.
——. Review of *Formule générale de l'histoire de tous les peuples appliquée à l'histoire du peuple Romain*, by Pierre Simon Ballanche, *Jahrbuch für wissenschaftliche Kritik*, 1836, pp. 641–55.

——. Review of *Geschichte des römischen Rechts im Mittelalter* (vol. 4), by Friedrich Carl von Savigny, *Jahrbuch für wissenschaftliche Kritik*, 1827, pp. 321–44.
——. Review of *Histoire de la révolution d'Angelterre depuis l'avénement de Charles I. jusqu'à la chute de Jacques II*, by François Pierre Guillaume Guizot, *Jahrbuch für wissenschaftliche Kritik*, 1828, pp. 467–68.
——. Review of *Histoire des institutions de Moise, et du peuple Hebreu*, by J. Salvador, *Jahrbuch für wissenschaftliche Kritik*, 1830, pp. 941–44.
——. Review of *Historische Erinnerungen in lyrischen Gedichten*, by Friedrich August von Stägemann, *Jahrbuch für wissenschaftliche Kritik*, 1829, pp. 1–8.
——. Review of *Introduction à l'histoire universelle*, by Jules Michelet, *Jahrbuch für wissenschaftliche Kritik*, 1832, pp. 141–57.
——. Review of *Introduction génerale à l'histoire du droit*, by Eugène Lerminier, *Jahrbuch für wissenschaftliche Kritik*, 1830, pp. 629–40.
——. Review of *Les conflits ou empiètement de l'autorité administrative sur le pouvoir judiciaire*, by F.N. Bavoux, *Jahrbuch für wissenschaftliche Kritik*, 1828, pp. 467–78.
——. Review of *Manuel des consuls*, by Alexandre de Miltitz, *Jahrbuch für wissenschaftliche Kritik*, 1837, pp. 94–99.
——. Review of *Studien und Skizzen zu einer Naturlehre des Staates* (part 1), by Heinrich Leo, *Jahrbuch für wissenschaftliche Kritik*, 1833, pp. 701–08, 713–17.
——. Review of *The Constitutional History of England from the Accession of Henry VII to the Death of George II*, by Henry Hallam, *Jahrbuch für wissenschaftliche Kritik*, 1828, pp. 649–68.
——, Review of *Ueber die Restauration des deutschen Rechts, insbesondere in Beziehung auf das Grundeigenthum*, by Friedrich Ludwig Bernhard, *Jahrbuch für wissenschaftliche Kritik*, 1830, pp. 838–40.
——. Review of *Über die Unvereinbarkeit der hegelschen Staatslehre mit dem obersten Lebens- und Enwicklungsprinzip des preussischen Staates*, by K.E. Schubarth, *Jahrbuch für wissenschaftliche Kritik*, 1839, pp. 199–208. Reprinted as "Erwiderung auf Schubarth," in Riedel, Manfred. Ed. *Materialien zu Hegels Rechtsphilosophie*. Vol. 1. Frankfurt am Main: Suhrkamp, 1975. Pp. 267–75.
——. Review of *Über Verderbniss und Herstellung der Eidgenossenschaft*, by Severus Pertinax [pseud. I.P.V. Troxler], *Jahrbuch für wissenschaftliche Kritik*, 1833, pp. 59–63.
——. Review of *Übersichtliche Darstellung des preussischen Staatsrechts*, by Alexander Mirus, *Jahrbuch für wissenschaftliche Kritik*, 1833, pp. 183–84.
——. Review of *Versuch einer Darstellung der Geschichte des angelsächsischen Rechts*, by George Phillips, *Jahrbuch für wissenschaftliche Kritik*, 1827, pp. 107–20.
——. "A Society to Further Jewish Integration." ["Halbjährlicher Bericht".] Trans. J. Hessing. In *The Jew in the Modern World: A Documentary History*. Edited by Paul R. Mendes-Flohr and Jehuda Reinharz. New York: Oxford University Press, 1980. Pp. 190–93.
——. "Über die Untersuchungsmaxime des preussischen Zivilprozesses." In Gans, Eduard. Ed. *Beiträge zur Revision der preussischen Gesetzgebung* (Berlin 1832). Pp. 450–79. Reprinted in part (pages 468–78) in Waszek, Norbert, ed. *Eduard Gans (1797–1839): Hegelianer-Jude-Europäer: Texte und Dokumente*. Hegeliana: Studien und Quellen zu Hegel und zum Hegelianismus, vol. 1. Series edited by Helmut Schneider. Frankfurt am Main: Peter Lang, 1991. Pp. 147–155.
——. "Vorlesungen über die Geschichte der Juden im Norden von Europa und in den slavischen Ländern." *Zeitschrift für die Wissenschaft des Judentums* 1 (1822). Reprinted as "Über die Einwanderung der Juden in England." *Vermischte Schriften, juristischen, historischen, staatswissenschaftlichen und ästhetischen Inhalts*, vol. 2.
——. "Vorrede der Herausgegebers." [Preface to Hegel's Philosophy of History. See entry under editions.]

——. "Vorrede der Herausgegebers." [Preface to Hegel's *Philosophy of Law*. See entry under editions.]

[——, Moser, Moses, and Zunz, Leopold]. The Society for the Culture and Science of Jews: Statutes. In *The Jew in the Modern World" A Documentary History*. Edited by Paul R. Mendes-Flohr and Jehuda Reinharz. New York: Oxford University Press, 1980. Pp. 188–89.

Works edited by Gans

Gans, Eduard, ed. *Beiträge zur Revision der preussischen Gesetzgebung*. One volume in 6 parts. Berlin: Duncker und Humblot, 1830–32.

——, ed. *Georg Wilhelm Friedrich Hegel's Grundlinien der Philosophie des Rechts; oder Naturrecht und Staatswissenschaft im Grundrisse*. Georg Wilhelm Friedrich Hegel, *Georg Wilhelm Friedrich Hegel's Werke*, 18 vols., complete edition, edited by a Society of Friends of the Deceased, comprising Marheineke, Schulze, Gans, Henning, Hotho, Michelet, and Förster, (Berlin: Duncker und Humblot, 1832–45), vol. 8 (1833). Republished in 1840.

——, ed. *Georg Wilhelm Friedrich Hegel's Vorlesungen über die Philosophie der Geschichte*. Georg Wilhelm Friedrich Hegel, *Georg Wilhelm Friedrich Hegel's Werke*, 18 vols., complete edition, edited by a Society of Friends of the Deceased, comprising Marheineke, Schulze, Gans, Henning, Hotho, Michelet, and Förster, (Berlin: Duncker und Humblot, 1832–45), vol. 9 (1837).

——, ed. *Jahrbücher für wissenschaftliche Kritik*. Berlin: 1827–32.

COLLECTIONS AND CRITICAL EDITIONS

——. *Materialien zu den "Jahrbüchern für wissenschaftliche Kritik"*. Edited by Norbert Waszek. Spekulation und Erfahrung. Division 1, vol. 3. Frommann-Holzboog, 1994. [Forthcoming.]

——. *Naturrecht und Universalrechtsgeschichte*. Edited by Manfred Riedel. Deutscher Idealismus: Philosophie und Wirkungsgeschichte in Quellen und Studien, edited by Hans Michael Baumgartner, et al., vol. 2. Stuttgart: Klett-Cotta, 1981.

——. *Philosophische Schriften*. Edited with an Introduction by Horst Schröder. Glashütten im Taunus: Verlag Detlev Auvermann K.G., 1971.

Espagne, Michel, and Werner, Michael, eds. *Lettres d'Allemagne: Victor Cousin et les hégéliens*. Tusson, Charente: Du Lerot, 1990.

Waszek, Norbert, ed. *Eduard Gans (1797–1839): Hegelianer – Jude – Europäer: Texte und Dokumente*. Hegeliana: Studien und Quellen zu Hegel und zum Hegelianismus, edited by Helmut Schneider, vol. 1. Frankfurt am Main: Peter Lang, 1991.

WORKS ABOUT GANS

Books and Dissertations about Gans

Friedlander, Albert Hoschander. "The Verein für Kultur und Wissenschaft der Juden: A Study in the History of Culture. Rabbinical dissertation." Hebrew Union College-Jewish Institute of Religion, Cincinnati campus. 1952.

Reissner, Hanns Günther. *Eduard Gans: Ein Leben im Vormärz*. Schriftenreihe Wissenschaftlicher Abhandlungen des Leo Baeck Instituts, vol. 14. Tübingen: J.C.B. Mohr (Paul Siebeck), 1965.

Books that treat Gans

Lefebvre, Jean Pierre Lefebvre. *Der gute Trommler: Heines Beziehung zu Hegel.* Heine-Studien. Edited by Joseph a Kruse. Hamburg: Hoffmann und Campe, 1986.

Matassi, Elio, *Eredità hegeliane: Da Cieszkowski e Gans a Ritter.* Naples: Morano Editore, 1991.

S.S. Prawer. *Heine's Jewish Comedy: A Study of his Portraits of Jews and Judaism.* Oxford: Clarendon Press, 1983

Riedel, Manfred. *Between Tradition and Revolution: The Hegelian Transformation of Political Philosophy.* Translated by Walter Wright. Cambridge; Cambridge University Press, 1984.

Toews, John E. *Hegelianism: The Path toward Dialectical Humanism, 1805–1841.* Cambridge: Cambridge University Press, 1980.

Articles

Beyer, Wilhelm Raimund. "Gans' Vorrede zur hegelschen Rechtsphilosophie." *Archiv für Rechts- und Sozialphilosophie* 45 (1959): 257–73.

Braun, Johann. "Die '*lex Gans*' – ein Kapitel aus der Geschichte der Judenemanzipation in Preussen." *Zeitschrift der Savigny-Stiftung für Rechtsgeschichte.* Germanistische Abteilung 102 (1985): 60–98.

——, "Schwan und Gans." *Juristenzeitung* 34 (1979): 769–75.

Meist, Kurt Rainer. "Altenstein und Gans: Eine frühe politische Option für Hegels Rechtsphilosophie." *Hegel-Studien* 14 (1979): 39–72.

Riedel, Manfred. "Eduard Gans als Schüler Hegels: zur politischen Auslegung der Rechtsphilosophie." *Rivista di Filosofia* 68 (1977): 234–53. This article is a revised version of "Hegel und Gans," which is separately cited below.

——. "Eduard Gans, discepolo di Hegel. Per l'interpretazione politica dell filosofia del diritto." Trans. Gianstefano Villa. *Rivista di Filosofia* 68 (1977): 254–68. [Translation of the preceding title.]

——. "Hegel und Gans." In *Natur und Geschichte: Karl Loewith zum 70. Geburtstag.* Edited by Hermann Braun and Manfred Riedel. Stuttgart: Verlags Kohlhammer, 1967. Pp. 257–73.

Schorsch, Ismar. "The Religious Parameters of Wissenschaft: Jewish Academics at Prussian Universities." *Yearbook of the Leo Baeck Institute* 25 (1980): 3–19.

Schröder, Horst. "Zum Gedenken an Eduard Gans." *Wissenschaftliche Zeitschrift der Humboldt Universität zu Berlin: Gesellschafts- und Sprachwissenschaftliche Reihe* 13 (1964): 515–22.

Vaccaro, Giovambattista. "Hegelism e liberalism tra Eduard Gans e Arnold Ruge." *Annali della Fondazione Luigi Einaudi* 14 (1980): 331–77.

Waszek, Norbert. "Eduard Gans, die 'Jahrbücher für wissenschaftliche Kritik' und die französische Publizistik der Zeit." In *Die "Jahrbücher für wissenschaftliche Kritik": Hegels Berliner Gegenakademie.* Edited by Christoph Jamme. Frommann-Holzboog, 1994. Pp. 93–118.

——. "Eduard Gans on Poverty: Between Hegel and Saint-Simon." *Owl of Minerva* 18 (1987): 167–78.

——. "Eduard Gans und die Armut: Von Hegel und Saint-Simon zu frühgewerkschaftlichen Forderungen." Heinz Kimmerle, Wolfgang Lefèvre, and Rudolf W. Meyer, ed. *Hegel-Jahrbuch 1988.* Bochum: Germinal Verlag, 1988. Pp. 355–63.

——. "Eduard Gans' Briefe an Athanase Jourdan." *Hegel-Studien* 22 (1987): 25–44.

——. "Freiheit und Verfassung: Von Hegel zu Gans." *Archiv für Rechts- und Sozialphilosophie* 78 (1992): 460–71.

——. "La Réception du Saint-Simonisme dans l'école hégélienne: l'exemple d'Eduard Gans." *Archives de Philosophie* 52 (1989): 581–87.

——. "The Stagnation of the Consciousness of Freedom: A Challenge to Hegelianism." Henk Oosterling and Frans de Jong, ed. *Denken Unterwegs: Philosophie im Kräftefeld sozialen und politischen Engagements.* Festschrift für Heinz Kimmerle zu seinem 60. Geburtstag. Amsterdam: Verlag B.R. Grüner, 1990. Pp. 175–85.

——. "Zwischen Hegel und Marx: Eine Würdigung Eduard Gans' anlässlich der 150. Wiederkehr seines Todestages." *Dialektik* 17 (1989): 162–76.

SELECTED HISTORICAL STUDIES OF ROMAN AND GERMAN LEGAL HISTORY

Books

John, Michael. *Politics and Law in Late Nineteenth-Century Germany: The Origins of the Civil Code.* Oxford: Clarendon Press, 1989.

Johnston, David. *The Roman Law of Trusts.* Oxford: Clarendon Press, 1988.

Watson, Alan. *The Law of Succession in the Later Roman Republic.* Oxford: Clarendon Press, 1971.

Whitman, James Q. *The Legacy of Roman Law in the German Romantic Era: Historical Vision and Legal Change.* Princeton: Princeton University Press, 1990.

Wesenberg, Gerhard [and Wesener, Gunter]. *Neuere deutsche Privatrechtsgeschichte: im Rahmen der europäischen Rechtsentwicklung.* From the second edition of Gunter Wesener. 4th ed. Vienna: Hermann Böhlaus Nach., 1985.

Wieacker, Franz. *Privatrechtsgeschichte der Neuzeit: unter besonderer Berücksichtigung der deutschen Entwicklung.* 2d ed. Göttingen: Vandenhoeck & Ruprecht, 1967.

Law review articles

Buxbaum, Richard M. Editor-in-Chief. Symposium. "Savigny in Modern Comparative Perspective." *The American Journal of Comparative Law* 37 (1989): 1–69.

Gale, Susan Gaylord. "A Very German Legal Science: Savigny and the Historical School." *Stanford Journal of International Law* 18 (1982): 123–46.

Reimann, Mathias. "Nineteenth Century German Legal Science." *Boston College Law Review* 31 (1990): 837–97.

INDEX

ARCHIVES INTERNATIONALES D'HISTOIRE DES IDÉES
*
INTERNATIONAL ARCHIVES OF THE HISTORY OF IDEAS

1. E. Labrousse: *Pierre Bayle*. Tome I: *Du pays de foix à la cité d'Erasme*. 1963; 2nd printing 1984 ISBN 90-247-3136-4
   For Tome II *see below under Volume 6.*
2. P. Merlan: *Monopsychism, Mysticism, Metaconsciousness*. Problems of the Soul in the Neoaristotelian and Neoplatonic Tradition. 1963; 2nd printing 1969 ISBN 90-247-0178-3
3. H.G. van Leeuwen: *The Problem of Certainty in English Thought, 1630–1690*. With a Preface by R.H. Popkin. 1963; 2nd printing 1970 ISBN 90-247-0179-1
4. P.W. Janssen: *Les origines de la réforme des Carmes en France au 17e* Siècle. 1963; 2nd printing 1969 ISBN 90-247-0180-5
5. G. Sebba: *Bibliographia Cartesiana*. A Critical Guide to the Descartes Literature (1800–1960). 1964 ISBN 90-247-0181-3
6. E. Labrousse: *Pierre Bayle*. Tome II: *Heterodoxie et rigorisme*. 1964 ISBN 90-247-0182-1
7. K.W. Swart: *The Sense of Decadence in 19th-Century France*. 1964 ISBN 90-247-0183-X
8. W. Rex: *Essays on Pierre Bayle and Religious Controversy*. 1965 ISBN 90-247-0184-8
9. E. Heier: *L.H. Nicolay (1737-1820) and His Contemporaries*. Diderot, Rousseau, Voltaire, Gluck, Metastasio, Galiani, D'Escherny, Gessner, Bodmer, Lavater, Wieland, Frederick II, Falconet, W. Robertson, Paul I, Cagliostro, Gellert, Winckelmann, Poinsinet, Lloyd, Sanchez, Masson, and Others. 1965 ISBN 90-247-0185-6
10. H.M. Bracken: *The Early Reception of Berkeley's Immaterialism, 1710–1733*. [1958] Rev. ed. 1965 ISBN 90-247-0186-4
11. R.A. Watson: *The Downfall of Cartesianism, 1673–1712*. A Study of Epistemological Issues in Late 17th-Century Cartesianism. 1966 ISBN 90-247-0187-2
12. R. Descartes: *Regulæ ad Directionem Ingenii*. Texte critique établi par Giovanni Crapulli avec la version hollandaise du 17e siècle. 1966 ISBN 90-247-0188-0
13. J. Chapelain: *Soixante-dix-sept Lettres inédites à Nicolas Heinsius (1649-1658)*. Publiées d'après le manuscrit de Leyde avec une introduction et des notes par B. Bray. 1966 ISBN 90-247-0189-9
14. C. B. Brush: *Montaigne and Bayle*. Variations on the Theme of Skepticism. 1966 ISBN 90-247-0190-2
15. B. Neveu: *Un historien à l'Ecole de Port-Royal*. Sébastien le Nain de Tillemont (1637-1698). 1966 ISBN 90-247-0191-0
16. A. Faivre: *Kirchberger et l'Illuminisme du 18e* siècle. 1966 ISBN 90-247-0192-9
17. J.A. Clarke: *Huguenot Warrior*. The Life and Times of Henri de Rohan (1579-1638). 1966 ISBN 90-247-0193-7
18. S. Kinser: *The Works of Jacques-Auguste de Thou*. 1966 ISBN 90-247-0194-5
19. E.F. Hirsch: *Damião de Gois*. The Life and Thought of a Portuguese Humanist (1502-1574). 1967 ISBN 90-247-0195-3
20. P.J.S. Whitemore: *The Order of Minims in 17th-Century France*. 1967 ISBN 90-247-0196-1
21. H. Hillenaar: *Fénelon et les Jésuites*. 1967 ISBN 90-247-0197-X

ARCHIVES INTERNATIONALES D'HISTOIRE DES IDÉES
*
INTERNATIONAL ARCHIVES OF THE HISTORY OF IDEAS

22. W.N. Hargreaves-Mawdsley: *The English Della Cruscans and Their Time, 1783-1828.* 1967 ISBN 90-247-0198-8
23. C.B. Schmitt: *Gianfrancesco Pico della Mirandola (1469-1533) and his Critique of Aristotle.* 1967 ISBN 90-247-0199-6
24. H.B. White: *Peace among the Willows.* The Political Philosophy of Francis Bacon. 1968 ISBN 90-247-0200-3
25. L. Apt: *Louis-Philippe de Ségur.* An Intellectual in a Revolutionary Age. 1969 ISBN 90-247-0201-1
26. E.H. Kadler: *Literary Figures in French Drama (1784- 1834).* 1969 ISBN 90-247-0202-X
27. G. Postel: *Le Thrésor des prophéties de l'univers.* Manuscrit publié avec une introduction et des notes par F. Secret. 1969 ISBN 90-247-0203-8
28. E.G. Boscherini: *Lexicon Spinozanum.* 2 vols., 1970 Set ISBN 90-247-0205-4
29. C.A. Bolton: *Church Reform in 18th-Century Italy.* The Synod of Pistoia (1786). 1969 ISBN 90-247-0208-9
30. D. Janicaud: *Une généalogie du spiritualisme français.* Aux sources du bergsonisme: [Félix] Ravaisson [1813-1900] et la métaphysique. 1969 ISBN 90-247-0209-7
31. J.-E. d'Angers: *L'Humanisme chrétien au 17e siècle.* St. François de Sales et Yves de Paris. 1970 ISBN 90-247-0210-0
32. H.B. White: *Copp'd Hills towards Heaven.* Shakespeare and the Classical Polity. 1970 ISBN 90-247-0250-X
33. P.J. Olscamp: *The Moral Philosophy of George Berkeley.* 1970 ISBN 90-247-0303-4
34. C.G. Noreña: *Juan Luis Vives (1492-1540).* 1970 ISBN 90-247-5008-3
35. J. O'Higgens: *Anthony Collins (1676-1729), the Man and His World.* 1970 ISBN 90-247-5007-5
36. F.T. Brechka: *Gerard van Swieten and His World (1700- 1772).* 1970 ISBN 90-247-5009-1
37. M.H. Waddicor: *Montesquieu and the Pilosophy of Natural Law.* 1970 ISBN 90-247-5039-3
38. O.R. Bloch: *La Philosophie de Gassendi (1592-1655).* Nominalisme, matérialisme et métaphysique. 1971 ISBN 90-247-5035-0
39. J. Hoyles: *The Waning of the Renaissance (1640-1740).* Studies in the Thought and Poetry of Henry More, John Norris and Isaac Watts. 1971 ISBN 90-247-5077-6
    For Henry More, *see also below under Volume 122 and 127.*
40. H. Bots: *Correspondance de Jacques Dupuy et de Nicolas Heinsius (1646-1656).* 1971 ISBN 90-247-5092-X
41. W.C. Lehmann: *Henry Home, Lord Kames, and the Scottish Enlightenment.* A Study in National Character and in the History of Ideas. 1971 ISBN 90-247-5018-0
42. C. Kramer: *Emmery de Lyere et Marnix de Sainte Aldegonde.* Un admirateur de Sébastien Franck et de Montaigne aux prises avec le champion des calvinistes néerlandais.[Avec le texte d'Emmery de Lyere:] *Antidote ou contrepoison contre les conseils sanguinaires et envinemez de Philippe de Marnix Sr. de Ste. Aldegonde.* 1971 ISBN 90-247-5136-5

ARCHIVES INTERNATIONALES D'HISTOIRE DES IDÉES
*
INTERNATIONAL ARCHIVES OF THE HISTORY OF IDEAS

43. P. Dibon: *Inventaire de la correspondance (1595-1650) d'André Rivet (1572-1651).* 1971 ISBN 90-247-5112-8
44. K.A. Kottman: *Law and Apocalypse.* The Moral Thought of Luis de Leon (1527?-1591). 1972 ISBN 90-247-1183-5
45. F.G. Nauen: *Revolution, Idealism and Human Freedom.* Schelling, Hölderlin and Hegel, and the Crisis of Early German Idealism. 1971 ISBN 90-247-5117-9
46. H. Jensen: *Motivation and the Moral Sense in Francis Hutcheson's* [1694-1746] *Ethical Theory.* 1971 ISBN 90-247-1187-8
47. A. Rosenberg: *[Simon] Tyssot de Patot and His Work (1655–1738).* 1972 ISBN 90-247-1199-1
48. C. Walton: *De la recherche du bien.* A study of [Nicolas de] Malebranche's [1638-1715] Science of Ethics. 1972 ISBN 90-247-1205-X
49. P.J.S. Whitmore (ed.): *A 17th-Century Exposure of Superstition.* Select Text of Claude Pithoys (1587-1676). 1972 ISBN 90-247-1298-X
50. A. Sauvy: *Livres saisis à Paris entre 1678 et 1701.* D'après une étude préliminaire de Motoko Ninomiya. 1972 ISBN 90-247-1347-1
51. W.R. Redmond: *Bibliography of the Philosophy in the Iberian Colonies of America.* 1972 ISBN 90-247-1190-8
52. C.B. Schmitt: *Cicero Scepticus.* A Study of the Influence of the *Academica* in the Renaissance. 1972 ISBN 90-247-1299-8
53. J. Hoyles: *The Edges of Augustanism.* The Aesthetics of Spirituality in Thomas Ken, John Byrom and William Law. 1972 ISBN 90-247-1317-X
54. J. Bruggeman and A.J. van de Ven (éds.): *Inventaire* des pièces d'Archives françaises se rapportant à l'Abbaye de Port-Royal des Champs et son cercle et à la Résistance contre la Bulle *Unigenitus* et à l'Appel. 1972 ISBN 90-247-5122-5
55. J.W. Montgomery: *Cross and, Crucible.* Johann Valentin Andreae (1586–1654), Phoenix of the Theologians. Volume I: Andreae's Life, World-View, and Relations with Rosicrucianism and Alchemy; Volume II: The *Chymische Hochzeit* with Notes and Commentary. 1973 Set ISBN 90-247-5054-7
56. O. Lutaud: *Des révolutions d'Angleterre à la Révolution française.* Le tyrannicide & *Killing No Murder* (Cromwell, *Athalie*, Bonaparte). 1973 ISBN 90-247-1509-1
57. F. Duchesneau: *L'Empirisme de Locke.* 1973 ISBN 90-247-1349-8
58. R. Simon (éd.): *Henry de Boulainviller* - Œuvres Philosophiques, Tome I. 1973 ISBN 90-247-1332-3

    For Œvres Philosophiques, Tome II *see below under Volume 70.*
59. E.E. Harris: *Salvation from Despair.* A Reappraisal of Spinoza's Philosophy. 1973 ISBN 90-247-5158-6
60. J.-F. Battail: *L'Avocat philosophe Géraud de Cordemoy (1626-1684).* 1973 ISBN 90-247-1542-3
61. T. Liu: *Discord in Zion.* The Puritan Divines and the Puritan Revolution (1640-1660). 1973 ISBN 90-247-5156-X
62. A. Strugnell: *Diderot's Politics.* A Study of the Evolution of Diderot's Political Thought after the *Encyclopédie.* 1973 ISBN 90-247-1540-7

ARCHIVES INTERNATIONALES D'HISTOIRE DES IDÉES
*
INTERNATIONAL ARCHIVES OF THE HISTORY OF IDEAS

63. G. Defaux: *Pantagruel et les Sophistes.* Contribution à l'histoire de l'humanisme chrétien au 16e siècle. 1973 ISBN 90-247-1566-0
64. G. Planty-Bonjour: *Hegel et la pensée philosophique en Russie (1830-1917).* 1974 ISBN 90-247-1576-8
65. R.J. Brook: [*George*] *Berkeley's Philosophy of Science.* 1973 ISBN 90-247-1555-5
66. T.E. Jessop: *A Bibliography of George Berkeley.* With: *Inventory of Berkeley's Manuscript Remains* by A.A. Luce. 2nd revised and enlarged ed. 1973 ISBN 90-247-1577-6
67. E.I. Perry: *From Theology to History.* French Religious Controversy and the Revocation of the Edict of Nantes. 1973 ISBN 90-247-1578-4
68. P. Dibbon, H. Bots et E. Bots-Estourgie: *Inventaire de la correspondance (1631–1671) de Johannes Fredericus Gronovius* [1611–1671]. 1974 ISBN 90-247-1600-4
69. A.B. Collins: *The Secular is Sacred.* Platonism and Thomism in Marsilio Ficino's *Platonic Theology.* 1974 ISBN 90-247-1588-1
70. R. Simon (éd.): *Henry de Boulainviller.* Œuvres Philosophiques, Tome II. 1975 ISBN 90-247-1633-0

    For Œvres Philosophiques, Tome I *see under Volume 58.*
71. J.A.G. Tans et H. Schmitz du Moulin: *Pasquier Quesnel devant la Congrégation de l'Index.* Correspondance avec Francesco Barberini et mémoires sur la mise à l'Index de son édition des Œuvres de Saint Léon, publiés avec introduction et annotations. 1974 ISBN 90-247-1661-6
72. J.W. Carven: *Napoleon and the Lazarists (1804–1809).* 1974 ISBN 90-247-1667-5
73. G. Symcox: *The Crisis of French Sea Power (1688–1697).* From the *Guerre d'Escadre* to the *Guerre de Course.* 1974 ISBN 90-247-1645-4
74. R. MacGillivray: *Restoration Historians and the English Civil War.* 1974 ISBN 90-247-1678-0
75. A. Soman (ed.): *The Massacre of St. Bartholomew.* Reappraisals and Documents. 1974 ISBN 90-247-1652-7
76. R.E. Wanner: *Claude Fleury (1640-1723) as an Educational Historiographer and Thinker.* With an Introduction by W.W. Brickman. 1975 ISBN 90-247-1684-5
77. R.T. Carroll: *The Common-Sense Philosophy of Religion of Bishop Edward Stillingfleet (1635-1699).* 1975 ISBN 90-247-1647-0
78. J. Macary: *Masque et lumières au 18e [siècle].* André-François Deslandes, Citoyen et philosophe (1689-1757). 1975 ISBN 90-247-1698-5
79. S.M. Mason: *Montesquieu's Idea of Justice.* 1975 ISBN 90-247-1670-5
80. D.J.H. van Elden: *Esprits fins et esprits géométriques dans les portraits de Saint-Simon.* Contributions à l'étude du vocabulaire et du style. 1975 ISBN 90-247-1726-4
81. I. Primer (ed.): *Mandeville Studies.* New Explorations in the Art and Thought of Dr Bernard Mandeville (1670-1733). 1975 ISBN 90-247-1686-1
82. C.G. Noreña: *Studies in Spanish Renaissance Thought.* 1975 ISBN 90-247-1727-2
83. G. Wilson: *A Medievalist in the 18th Century.* Le Grand d'Aussy and the Fabliaux ou Contes. 1975 ISBN 90-247-1782-5
84. J.-R. Armogathe: *Theologia Cartesiana.* L'explication physique de l'Eucharistie chez Descartes et Dom Robert Desgabets. 1977 ISBN 90-247-1869-4

ARCHIVES INTERNATIONALES D'HISTOIRE DES IDÉES
*
INTERNATIONAL ARCHIVES OF THE HISTORY OF IDEAS

85. Bérault Stuart, Seigneur d'Aubigny: *Traité sur l'art de la guerre.* Introduction et édition par Élie de Comminges. 1976 ISBN 90-247-1871-6
86. S.L. Kaplan: *Bread, Politics and Political Economy in the Reign of Louis XV.* 2 vols., 1976 Set ISBN 90-247-1873-2
87. M. Lienhard (ed.): *The Origins and Characteristics of Anabaptism / Les débuts et les caractéristiques de l'Anabaptisme.* With an Extensive Bibliography / Avec une bibliographie détaillée. 1977 ISBN 90-247-1896-1
88. R. Descartes: *Règles utiles et claires pour la direction de l'esprit en la recherche de la vérité.* Traduction selon le lexique cartésien, et annotation conceptuelle par J.-L. Marion. Avec des notes mathématiques de P. Costabel. 1977 ISBN 90-247-1907-0
89. K. Hardesty: *The 'Supplément' to the 'Encyclopédie'.* [Diderot et d'Alembert]. 1977 ISBN 90-247-1965-8
90. H.B. White: *Antiquity Forgot.* Essays on Shakespeare, [Francis] Bacon, and Rembrandt. 1978 ISBN 90-247-1971-2
91. P.B.M. Blaas: *Continuity and Anachronism.* Parliamentary and Constitutional Development in Whig Historiography and in the Anti-Whig Reaction between 1890 and 1930. 1978 ISBN 90-247-2063-X
92. S.L. Kaplan (ed.): *La Bagarre.* Ferdinando Galiani's (1728-1787) 'Lost' Parody. With an Introduction by the Editor. 1979 ISBN 90-247-2125-3
93. E. McNiven Hine: *A Critical Study of [Étienne Bonnot de] Condillac's* [1714-1780] *'Traité des Systèmes'.* 1979 ISBN 90-247-2120-2
94. M.R.G. Spiller: *Concerning Natural Experimental Philosphy.* Meric Casaubon [1599-1671] and the Royal Society. 1980 ISBN 90-247-2414-7
95. F. Duchesneau: *La physiologie des Lumières.* Empirisme, modèles et théories. 1982 ISBN 90-247-2500-3
96. M. Heyd: *Between Orthodoxy and the Enlightenment.* Jean-Robert Chouet [1642-1731] and the Introduction of Cartesian Science in the Academy of Geneva. 1982 ISBN 90-247-2508-9
97. James O'Higgins: *Yves de Vallone* [1666/7-1705]: *The Making of an Esprit Fort.* 1982 ISBN 90-247-2520-8
98. M.L. Kuntz: *Guillaume Postel* [1510-1581]. Prophet of the Restitution of All Things. His Life and Thought. 1981 ISBN 90-247-2523-2
99. A. Rosenberg: *Nicolas Gueudeville and His Work (1652-172?).* 1982 ISBN 90-247-2533-X
100. S.L. Jaki: *Uneasy Genius: The Life and Work of Pierre Duhem* [1861-1916]. 1984 ISBN 90-247-2897-5; Pb (1987) 90-247-3532-7
101. Anne Conway [1631-1679]: *The Principles of the Most Ancient Modern Philosophy.* Edited and with an Introduction by P. Loptson. 1982 ISBN 90-247-2671-9
102. E.C. Patterson: *[Mrs.] Mary [Fairfax Greig] Sommerville* [1780-1872] *and the Cultivation of Science (1815-1840).* 1983 ISBN 90-247-2823-1
103. C.J. Berry: *Hume, Hegel and Human Nature.* 1982 ISBN 90-247-2682-4
104. C.J. Betts: *Early Deism in France.* From the so-called 'déistes' of Lyon (1564) to Voltaire's 'Lettres philosophiques' (1734). 1984 ISBN 90-247-2923-8

ARCHIVES INTERNATIONALES D'HISTOIRE DES IDÉES
*
INTERNATIONAL ARCHIVES OF THE HISTORY OF IDEAS

---

105. R. Gascoigne: *Religion, Rationality and Community.* Sacred and Secular in the Thought of Hegel and His Critics. 1985 ISBN 90-247-2992-0
106. S. Tweyman: *Scepticism and Belief in Hume's 'Dialogues Concerning Natural Religion'.* 1986 ISBN 90-247-3090-2
107. G. Cerny: *Theology, Politics and Letters at the Crossroads of European Civilization.* Jacques Basnage [1653-1723] and the Baylean Huguenot Refugees in the Dutch Republic. 1987 ISBN 90-247-3150-X
108. Spinoza's *Algebraic Calculation of the Rainbow & Calculation of Changes.* Edited and Translated from Dutch, with an Introduction, Explanatory Notes and an Appendix by M.J. Petry. 1985 ISBN 90-247-3149-6
109. R.G. McRae: *Philosophy and the Absolute.* The Modes of Hegel's Speculation. 1985 ISBN 90-247-3151-8
110. J.D. North and J.J. Roche (eds.): *The Light of Nature.* Essays in the History and Philosophy of Science presented to A.C. Crombie. 1985 ISBN 90-247-3165-8
111. C. Walton and P.J. Johnson (eds.): *[Thomas] Hobbes's 'Science of Natural Justice'.* 1987 ISBN 90-247-3226-3
112. B.W. Head: *Ideology and Social Science.* Destutt de Tracy and French Liberalism. 1985 ISBN 90-247-3228-X
113. A.Th. Peperzak: *Philosophy and Politics.* A Commentary on the Preface to Hegel's *Philosophy of Right.* 1987 ISBN Hb 90-247-3337-5; Pb ISBN 90-247-3338-3
114. S. Pines and Y. Yovel (eds.): *Maimonides* [1135-1204] *and Philosophy.* Papers Presented at the 6th Jerusalem Philosophical Encounter (May 1985). 1986 ISBN 90-247-3439-8
115. T.J. Saxby: *The Quest for the New Jerusalem, Jean de Labadie* [1610-1674] *and the Labadists (1610-1744).* 1987 ISBN 90-247-3485-1
116. C.E. Harline: *Pamphlets, Printing, and Political Culture in the Early Dutch Republic.* 1987 ISBN 90-247-3511-4
117. R.A. Watson and J.E. Force (eds.): *The Sceptical Mode in Modern Philosophy.* Essays in Honor of Richard H. Popkin. 1988 ISBN 90-247-3584-X
118. R.T. Bienvenu and M. Feingold (eds.): *In the Presence of the Past.* Essays in Honor of Frank Manuel. 1991 ISBN 0-7923-1008-X
119. J. van den Berg and E.G.E. van der Wall (eds.): *Jewish-Christian Relations in the 17th Century.* Studies and Documents. 1988 ISBN 90-247-3617-X
120. N. Waszek: *The Scottish Enlightenment and Hegel's Account of 'Civil Society'.* 1988 ISBN 90-247-3596-3
121. J. Walker (ed.): *Thought and Faith in the Philosophy of Hegel.* 1991 ISBN 0-7923-1234-1
122. Henry More [1614-1687]: *The Immortality of the Soul.* Edited with Introduction and Notes by A. Jacob. 1987 ISBN 90-247-3512-2
123. P.B. Scheurer and G. Debrock (eds.): *Newton's Scientific and Philosophical Legacy.* 1988 ISBN 90-247-3723-0
124. D.R. Kelley and R.H. Popkin (eds.): *The Shapes of Knowledge from the Renaissance to the Enlightenment.* 1991 ISBN 0-7923-1259-7

ARCHIVES INTERNATIONALES D'HISTOIRE DES IDÉES
*
INTERNATIONAL ARCHIVES OF THE HISTORY OF IDEAS

125. R.M. Golden (ed.): *The Huguenot Connection.* The Edict of Nantes, Its Revocation, and Early French Migration to South Carolina. 1988 ISBN 90-247-3645-5
126. S. Lindroth: *Les chemins du savoir en Suède.* De la fondation de l'Université d'Upsal à Jacob Berzelius. Études et Portraits. Traduit du suédois, présenté et annoté par J.-F. Battail. Avec une introduction sur Sten Lindroth par G. Eriksson. 1988 ISBN 90-247-3579-3
127. S. Hutton (ed.): *Henry More (1614-1687). Tercentenary Studies.* With a Biography and Bibliography by R. Crocker. 1989 ISBN 0-7923-0095-5
128. Y. Yovel (ed.): *Kant's Practical Philosophy Reconsidered.* Papers Presented at the 7th Jerusalem Philosophical Encounter (December 1986). 1989 ISBN 0-7923-0405-5
129. J.E. Force and R.H. Popkin: *Essays on the Context, Nature, and Influence of Isaac Newton's Theology.* 1990 ISBN 0-7923-0583-3
130. N. Capaldi and D.W. Livingston (eds.): *Liberty in Hume's 'History of England'.* 1990 ISBN 0-7923-0650-3
131. W. Brand: *Hume's Theory of Moral Judgment.* A Study in the Unity of *A Treatise of Human Nature.* 1992 ISBN 0-7923-1415-8
132. C.E. Harline (ed.): *The Rhyme and Reason of Politics in Early Modern Europe.* Collected Essays of Herbert H. Rowen. 1992 ISBN 0-7923-1527-8
133. N. Malebranche: *Treatise on Ethics* (1684). Translated and edited by C. Walton. 1993 ISBN 0-7923-1763-7
134. B.C. Southgate: *'Covetous of Truth'.* The Life and Work of Thomas White (1593–1676). 1993 ISBN 0-7923-1926-5
135. G. Santinello, C.W.T. Blackwell and Ph. Weller (eds.): *Models of the History of Philosophy.* Vol. 1: From its Origins in the Renaissance to the 'Historia Philosphica'. 1993 ISBN 0-7923-2200-2
136. M.J. Petry (ed.): *Hegel and Newtonianism.* 1993 ISBN 0-7923-2202-9
137. Otto von Guericke: *The New (so-called Magdeburg) Experiments* [Experimenta Nova, Amsterdam 1672]. Translated and edited by M.G.Foley Ames. 1994 ISBN 0-7923-2399-8
138. R.H. Popkin and G.M. Weiner (eds.): *Jewish Christians and Cristian Jews.* From the Renaissance to the Enlightenment. 1994 ISBN 0-7923-2452-8
139. J.E. Force and R.H. Popkin (eds.): *The Books of Nature and Scripture.* Recent Essays on Natural Philosophy, Theology, and Biblical Criticism in the Netherlands of Spinoza's Time and the British Isles of Newton's Time. 1994 ISBN 0-7923-2467-6
140. P. Rattansi and A. Clericuzio (eds.): *Alchemy and Chemistry in the 16th and 17th Centuries.* 1994 ISBN 0-7923-2573-7
141. S. Jayne: *Plato in Renaissance England.* 1995 ISBN 0-7923-3060-9
142. A.P. Coudert: *Leibniz and the Kabbalah.* 1995 ISBN 0-7923-3114-1
143. M.H. Hoffheimer: *Eduard Gans and the Hegelian Philosophy of Law.* 1995 ISBN 0-7923-3114-1

KLUWER ACADEMIC PUBLISHERS – DORDRECHT / BOSTON / LONDON

GPSR Compliance

The European Union's (EU) General Product Safety Regulation (GPSR) is a set of rules that requires consumer products to be safe and our obligations to ensure this.

If you have any concerns about our products, you can contact us on ProductSafety@springernature.com

In case Publisher is established outside the EU, the EU authorized representative is:

Springer Nature Customer Service Center GmbH
Europaplatz 3
69115 Heidelberg, Germany

Batch number: 10823775

Printed by Printforce, the Netherlands